No Longer Forgotten:
The
Remarkable Story
of
Christian Women's Job Corps

No Longer Forgotten:
The
Remarkable Story
of
Christian Women's Job Corps

Compiled by Charlene J. Gray
Edited by Trudy O. Johnson
With contributions
by
Evelyn Blount
C. Anne Davis
Dellanna O'Brien

New Hope Publishers
Birmingham, Alabama

New Hope Publishers
P.O. Box 12065
Birmingham, AL 35202-2065

Dewey Decimal Classification: 361.7
Subject Headings: CHURCH AND SOCIAL WORK
                  CHURCH WORK WITH WOMEN
                  PUBLIC WELFARE
                  MENTORING
                  CHRISTIAN WOMEN'S JOB CORPS
                  WOMAN'S MISSIONARY UNION, SBC

Scripture quotations identified CEV from Contemporary English Version.
© American Bible Society 1991. Used by permission.
Scripture taken from the NEW AMERICAN STANDARD BIBLE ®, © The
Lockman Foundation 1960, 1962, 1963, 1968, 1971, 1972, 1973, 1975,
1977. Used by permission.
Scripture quotations from the Revised Standard Version, © 1946, 1971,
1973 by the Division of Christian Education of the National Council of
the Churches of Christ in the U.S.A.
Scripture quotations from *The Message*. © 1993, 1994, 1995. Used by
permission of NavPress Publishing Group.

Cover design by Scott Miller
Photography by Lisa Braswell

ISBN: 1-56309-250-6
N984106 • 0698 • 5M1

To order products from New Hope Publishers or for a free catalog, call
1-800-968-7301. Also, visit our Web site at **newhopepubl.com**.

To Mindy, Linda, TJ, Camille, Dorothy, Elizabeth, Evelyn, Brenda, Gloria, Dusty, Diane, and Creely—for being my eyes and ears as I sorted through manuals, audio and video interviews, observational notes, and telephone notes. God smiles because of you.

To Cindy McClain—who walked with me through this unfolding project as a friend and guide.

To Brad, my husband—who withstood the demands of my writing, and made his mark by finding a meaningful way to channel resources for CWJC in Bismarck.

To Hunter—so that you will continue learning about God's world and what part He wants you to play.

To my family—for patiently waiting for phone calls and emails, and encouraging me with your prayers.

This book is dedicated to my sisters, Judi and Suzi, who have thrived against all odds.

Charlene J. Gray
Compiler

I DO NOT KNOW what it is like to be in need. In fact, for two decades I have conducted workshops on world hunger across the US, leading participants to declare with me: *I am rich by the world's standards!*

My life has been enriched by friendships with people who were in need. Growing up in south Florida, the annual return of seasonal farm workers brought Armando and Maria into my life. I looked forward to seeing them again year after year. They offered me the one gift they could afford, their friendship. And they helped me begin to glimpse what it is like to be in need.

For as long as I can remember, I have seen people in need and wanted to be a change agent in their lives. In a quest to understand those trapped in a cycle of poverty, residents of "less affluent" communities of Miami, Florida; Macon, Georgia; Louisville, Kentucky; Detroit, Michigan; and Phoenix, Arizona, have been my teachers. My passion for Christian Women's Job Corps (CWJC) and for communicating the hope of this vital ministry is attributable to these countless precious people. This dedication is a thank-you to them.

Nothing I have ever undertaken would have been possible without the lifelong support and encouragement of my mother. My forever best friend, she is the wind beneath my wings.

Confronting the number and types of needs CWJC participants have can be overwhelming. I am blessed to have a wonderful son, A.J., who provides me with joy that brings balance in my life. How I wish my legacy to him could be a world with less human need.

CWJC is in its infancy. What a privilege it has been to be a part of the birthing process! Nurturing the "baby" and watching her grow has led me to conclude that women in need are truly no longer forgotten! To the readers of this book, thank you for the chance to share the remarkable story of Christian Women's Job Corps with you.

Trudy Johnson
Editor

CONTENTS

FOREWORD
FROM THE EDITOR

CAN YOU TELL ME about Christian Women's Job Corps℠? It would be almost impossible to calculate how many times a day that question is asked. Inquiries come from women who are interested in ministering to women in need. And the investigations come from women in need as well as their concerned mothers, sisters, aunts, and grandmothers. Pastors and lay leaders who are seeking solutions for women trapped in poverty are drawn to CWJC. What is Christian Women's Job Corps? An explanation can be gained from the purpose statement: *The purpose of Christian Women's Job Corps, a ministry of Woman's Missionary Union ®, is to provide a Christian context in which women in need are equipped for life and employment and to provide a missions context in which women help women.*

The word *hope* is the most effective word to describe the results of this ministry. It was a search for hope that led Cynthia Howard to Christian Women's Job Corps at the Johenning Baptist Community Center. Cynthia, in recovery from alcohol addiction, wanted more for herself and her four young children than the life she had been living. An opportunity to complete her GED, receive job training, and participate in life-skills classes offered hope to

Cynthia. In mid-December 1997, she registered for CWJC^{SM}.

On February 2, 1998, Cynthia closed the door of her apartment in the bowels of our nation's capital and braced herself for walking in the frosty winter morning. Despite the cold, there was a joyful lilt in Cynthia's step, attributed to the fact she was on her way to CWJC at Johenning. Cynthia was casually dressed, had taken care in putting on makeup, and had her hair fashionably styled. It was going to be a special day for Cynthia!

The GED class for the day was science. The specific topic for study was health-related issues. James Kennedy, educational program coordinator at Johenning, led the class that included a discussion on cholesterol. When he stated that cholesterol build-up in the arteries could lead to a heart attack or stroke, Cynthia spoke up. She confessed to having high cholesterol and admitted that she had been having chest pains. "I plan to see a doctor about the pains," she said.

At this point in the class, James felt the Holy Spirit leading him to talk about what happens when someone dies. It was a discussion that included an exploration of Romans 10:9–13 and the need for salvation. James explained that one must be certain her lifeline to God is not clogged, blocking an opportunity for eternal life. Several students, including Cynthia, commented on their understanding of their relationship with God. But Cynthia wanted more. She wanted to be sure she acknowledged Jesus Christ as her Savior, and she wanted eternal life. James and Cynthia prayed together to seal Cynthia's decision to become a Christian. Cynthia left her CWJC class that day with a new source of hope. At home later that afternoon, Cynthia Howard suffered a massive heart attack and died.

In just a few short months, CWJC changed Cynthia Howard. Before she left this life, she had a reason to hope in a bright future of self-sufficiency for herself and her children. When she died, she had the assurance of eternal life. The Cynthias of today are the reason Christian Women's Job Corps exists. As Christians, we are challenged to respond to their needs, bringing hope for a better tomorrow and the message of good news that will change a life for all eternity. Christian Women's Job Corps means that women in need are no longer forgotten.

INTRODUCTION

IF YOU COULD paint a portrait of love, what colors would you choose? What highlights of grace or shades of mercy would you use? These are the colors that cover the canvas of Christian Women's Job Corps^{SM}. The canvas is unfinished; it is a portrait in the making as each day splashes new colors and images absorbed in God's love, grace, and mercy. This painting has been created with acute awareness of the dynamic action of God. Even as you read this book, more colors and images unfold, revealing more fully the story of Christian Women's Job Corps. Despite the incompleteness it is a remarkable story, one that must be told because it is *good news!* And by reading the story, you may be able to bring your own palette to this portrait and discover the colors of God's love, grace, and mercy in your life.

It is no coincidence that Woman's Missionary Union®, a women's organization grounded in the missions heart of God, would reach out to women in need—women caught in the cycle of poverty, trapped in hopelessness, forgotten by society. But now they are *no longer forgotten*. Christian Women's Job Corps is a ministry project created by Woman's Missionary Union that provides a Christian context for women in need to become equipped for life and employment. It also provides an opportunity for missions through which women help women.

Self-respect, self-sufficiency, and hope are the goals of Christian Women's Job Corps. The program's objectives reflect these goals:
- to build healthy self-esteem for women;
- to challenge women to define life goals;
- to encourage women to move toward those goals by developing life skills;
- to offer women opportunities to hear and respond to the gospel;
- to render emotional and spiritual support through a mentoring program;
- to provide opportunities for completion of basic education;
- to furnish job training that will prepare women for the job market;
- to identify potential employers; and
- to extend opportunities for each woman to give back to Christian Women's Job Corps.

In order to reach these goals, each Christian Women's Job Corps site must have eight program elements. First, each site coordinator assigns a mentor for every client. In this setting a mentor is a tutor, guide, counselor, nurturer, spiritual encourager, and facilitator of dreams for someone trying to break the cycle of poverty. Mentors offer personal, functional, relational, and spiritual guidance to a client.

Second, a covenant guides each client/mentor. The covenant identifies the expectations that the mentor and client have for one another. It is an agreement that identifies responsibilities in the relationship that a client and mentor share.

Third, Bible study is an integral part of the mentor/client relationship. Many women have never had a chance to study the Bible one-on-one and discover the riches and strength from His Word. This Bible study experience is customized to fit the spiritual development of the client. It may be basic Bible study addressing key biblical principles, or it may challenge clients through Scripture memory.

Fourth, networking is critical as project coordinators, mentors, and volunteers access resources of time, money, people, and facilities to help clients. Christian Women's Job Corps does not desire to duplicate services that already exist; rather, it intends to coordinate those resources to maximize the client's potential.

Fifth, CWJC assesses each woman's physical, emotional, educational, and spiritual needs. The assessment occurs at the beginning of the Christian Women's Job Corps experience, and it continues as the mentor/client relationship develops.

Sixth, a state or local advisory council guides each Christian Women's Job Corps site. This council serves as a resource and sounding board for CWJC volunteers as they strategize for effective ministry. Often they are the hands, heart, and feet of the ministry of Christian Women's Job Corps. Their spiritual resources are vital to the developing ministry.

Seventh, every site must have at least one person who has gone through Christian Women's Job Corps certification/training. This training is available through state or national WMU.

Finally, each Christian Women's Job Corps site must conduct ongoing evaluation of the project. This ensures continuing refinement of the ministry in order to meet the changing needs of clients.

Each of these program elements is developed to fit the site's needs and resources. For example, one site offers a ten-week job training course and then matches students with mentors. Another site offers one-on-one mentoring to meet ongoing educational needs with community resources. All of these models offer Bible study with mentors, so women can draw strength from God's Word as they develop self-esteem and confidence.

Customized program elements underscore that CWJC is no cookie-cutter ministry project. Christian Women's Job Corps volunteers design ministries for women who are suffering. The ministries always include loving them one by one, helping them up when they falter, accepting their failures, celebrating their successes, and teaching them where they are, as they are. Is this not the essence of God's loving grace? In truth, He takes us all as we are and where we are, regardless of our life circumstances. He is truly *Immanuel*—God with us.

Christian Women's Job Corps is a holistic ministry addressing the physical, emotional, social, financial, and spiritual needs of women who have no hope, no place to turn. This ministry calls Christian women to gather resources of time, money, spiritual gifts, and people from their church and community. It calls for women to grow in self-confidence as they move to self-sufficiency. Speaking at the first National Certification Training event, LaQuita Bell,

Christian Women's Job Corps project coordinator for Birmingham, Alabama, challenged WMU: "We have got to make people's needs our own. Affirm people's dignities. Give them back what God created them to have." The distinctive nature of Christian Women's Job Corps is that it provides a bridge for women who are homeless or in shelters to go from welfare to work.

This book paints a portrait of the remarkable story of Christian Women's Job Corps. Several authors paint their colors onto the canvas:

Trudy Johnson, Special Projects manager at Woman's Missionary Union, edited this book and gave firsthand insight into the life-changing stories of CWJC.

Dellanna O'Brien, executive director of Woman's Missionary Union, tells the history of CWJC.

Evelyn Blount, executive director of South Carolina Woman's Missionary Union, describes the rationale and context for women in poverty in the United States.

C. Anne Davis, retired professor and dean of the Carver School of Social Work at Southern Baptist Theological Seminary, creates the theological framework for CWJC.

As the compiler of this book, my task is to describe four of the pilot sites for Christian Women's Job Corps. They illustrate well the opportunities for custom-designed ministry that they face. Each Christian Women's Job Corps site has its own unique approach, style, history, culture, resources, and challenges. Each pilot site is charting its own course for mentoring and training. The constant for all sites is the unequivocal commitment of project coordinators and mentors to the spiritual development of participants through Bible study. This Bible study becomes an avenue for faith exploration and encounters with the Living Lord.

Each chapter describes the setting and the resources God is using through Christian Women's Job Corps and some of the women who are being touched through CWJC.

This story has no ending. Each day new challenges and opportunities emerge for project coordinators, mentors, and clients. Thus, the story will continue to unfold. In a world where many of these women of poverty live in the shadows, they frame their own stories with their own words. As you read, allow yourself to feel their pain and experience their triumphs. *They* are the story.

Throughout the book, you will see that each site identifies the

Christian Women's Job Corps participants with different terminology: *clients*, *students*, or *participants*. This demonstrates the unique approach each site is taking.

The sites described in this book are:

• Uptown Baptist Church in Chicago, Illinois—a church-based Christian Women's Job Corps site

• Bismarck, North Dakota—a community center-based Christian Women's Job Corps site

• San Antonio Baptist Association—an associational site housed at Riverside Baptist Church

• South Carolina—a state Christian Women's Job Corps project manifested in an associational site (York County).

The final chapter looks to the future of Christian Women's Job Corps and how two projects are currently being launched. They serve as examples of the dynamic process involved in setting up a project.

Since the first National Certification Training for Christian Women's Job Corps in August 1996, many states are launching their own ministries through Christian Women's Job Corps such as Grover Beach, California, and Nashville, Tennessee. Their stories bring new intensity to the portrait of Christian Women's Job Corps as God continues to call out workers to the harvest. He is the One Who calls and equips Christians for service.

My own journey of uncovering the Christian Women's Job Corps story has challenged me to reflect on the stewardship of God's grace and mercy in my life. I realize now that my life circumstances have little to do with my worth, and much to do with God's grace and mercy. This book is the first step of stewardship for me to share the story that I have seen, heard, and felt. My prayer is that Jesus Christ, the Master Painter, will use the portrait's story to challenge others to respond to God's call in their lives.

Charlene J. Gray
Compiler

1

....

In the Beginning:
A History of
Christian Women's Job Corps

IN THE BEGINNING:
A HISTORY OF CHRISTIAN WOMEN'S JOB CORPS
by Dellanna O'Brien

ON JULY 7, 1994, women characterized as being in need went about their daily routines not knowing that a meeting was taking place in Dallas, Texas, which could change their lives. For two days the Baptist General Convention of Texas offices provided the setting for the strategic meeting where the concept of Christian Women's Job Corps℠ was first discussed.

Who do we have to thank for the vision of a program to provide life and job skills training to women trapped in the cycle of poverty? Evelyn Blount, executive director of South Carolina Woman's Missionary Union (WMU); Joy Fenner, executive director of Texas WMU; Elmin Howell, Texas River Ministry director; Pat Luttrell, Texas WMU staff; Carolyn Miller, then national WMU president; Andrea Mullins, national WMU staff; Dellanna O'Brien, national WMU executive director; Jim Queen, director of missions, Chicago, Illinois; Frances Shaw, Florida WMU staff; Camille Simmons, San Antonio Baptist Association staff; and Evelyn Tully, executive director of Illinois WMU. This group formed the first CWJC National Task Force.

God's inspiration and leadership in the development of CWJC can be well documented. As is so often the case, He

chose to draw back the curtain on His plan through a series
of seemingly unrelated events.

A PROVOCATIVE PLUNGE

IN SEPTEMBER 1993, a group of WMU publication staff
members learned firsthand the unique challenge of ministry
in Chicago through an "Urban Plunge" arranged by the
North American Mission Board (formerly Home Mission
Board). The purpose was to observe and experience life in the
city for special emphases in our publications. We visited
churches of all sizes and descriptions, talked to missionaries
working in apartment and hospital settings, and heard the
heartaches and victories of witnessing to gang members and
drug and alcohol abusers in urban areas. The week served its
purpose in sensitizing us to what it takes to win our cities for
Christ.

The city's greatest need is, of course, for Christ and the
new life He gives. This is the urgent call of the city. In addition to this, our hearts were drawn to the multitude of
women, many of them mothers on welfare, caught in the trap
of poverty and unable to escape without someone's help. We
realized that the welfare cycle will continue to be operative in
our society until and unless someone begins to intervene in
individuals' lives.

AN INSPIRING IMMERSION

ONLY WEEKS AFTER the trip to Chicago, a group of state
WMU executive directors were joined by members of a task
force from Project HELP: Hunger, a social ministry project of
WMU. Their goal was to identify causes and effects of hunger
in our own country. While we were all reasonably aware of
the extent to which Americans suffer from economic oppres-
sion, the suffering became devastatingly clear as we saw it for
ourselves.

Once again, we saw women and children hopelessly
entangled in relationships and conditions that were seemingly insurmountable. In the shacks tucked away in the "little
hollers," living in unbelievable deprivation, were those who
considered themselves fortunate to have only the barest
necessities, eking out a mere existence. When one child in five

in our own land of plenty lives in poverty, something is wrong. The urgency of the situation caused us to ask, "Is there something WMU can do to help to relieve the suffering of women in poverty like this?"

We were very much aware that Chicago and Appalachia are not the only areas where women are trapped in poverty. During the following weeks and months this question haunted many of us: *Isn't there something we can do?* The question became a call and a challenge.

Our forays into these two very different environments made abundantly clear that, whether city or countryside, a growing pocket of poverty was evident—women, primarily single parents and welfare recipients.

Most of these women are unable to extricate themselves from the grip of poverty without help. They generally have few skills, little or no work experience, and no hope of breaking out of the welfare cycle. Yet these are women greatly loved by our Father, much like the outcasts and homeless to whom Christ reached out during His life and ministry here on Earth.

Our desire for more specific information sent us to demographic studies of women in poverty. We learned much in the early months of 1994, confirming the fact that the needs of many women in our land are staggering.

We had no doubt that there was a need for a Christian ministry to women in poverty, and it was an urgent need. But what would it take to assist women in their struggle out of despair into economic sufficiency?

WHAT WILL IT TAKE?

ONCE AGAIN GOD pulled back the curtain a bit on His plan for Christian Women's Job Corps. In the spring of 1994, following an associational meeting in a southern state, a director of missions drove me to the airport. He shared his life story easily, as though he had done it many times before.

He had grown up poor in the very area he now served. His father had been killed while he and a number of his siblings were still very young, leaving his mother to rear her children without benefit of insurance or Social Security payments.

In order to secure a job, the new widow moved to town, to live in a little house just a block away from a Baptist church. Although his mother never felt she had clothes nice enough to go to church, this director of missions as a child found the church members to be a second family. He ultimately accepted Christ as his Savior in this loving, nurturing situation.

When it was time for the young man to graduate from high school, one of the women in the church asked him what he planned to do. His response was quick—he would work for a year to save money to go to college. "Would you believe," he said, still astonished at his good fortune even after a number of years, "They helped send me to four years of college, even providing many of my clothes."

Then he became more somber, like a sage preparing to share his wisdom. "Those church folks made the difference in my life. You know it takes four things to get someone out of poverty.

"First, it takes someone to provide a stabilizing force. For me, it was just the right person in the church to meet the needs of the moment. The people in that church exemplified the mature, Christian walk throughout my impressionable years.

"Second, you must have some resources. Without the financial assistance, I might never have been able to complete my formal education. That would have seriously hindered my development.

"Third, you have to have hope—someone cheering you on from the sidelines, urging you on to new and even more demanding goals. Without the conviction that 'I can do this!' the rough times would have overcome any desire to pick up the pieces and try again. You have to have hope.

"And, finally, you have to have personal initiative. Others can assist and encourage, but unless the individual takes advantage of the help and becomes accountable for himself or herself, it will never happen."

Where were my paper and pen? This was the answer we had sought, the elements needed in assisting women out of the poverty cycle:

    1. A stabilizing influence.

2. Financial and human resources.
3. Hope.
4. Personal initiative.

These would need to be the components we would use in formulating our plan.

First Steps

THE JULY 1994 meeting produced both excitement and frustration. We were excited to be finally addressing the possibility of a tangible effort; after months of flirting with the issue, we were now actually taking concrete steps, albeit small ones. Pat Luttrell wrote a memo on July 15: "Thanks for letting me have a part in the groundbreaking for something BIG!" This was a common reaction for each of us.

The discussion was frustrating, however, because we had no model to follow, no guidelines to use. Thus, we brainstormed, dreamed, agonized, and grieved.

Some of us had studied the job market, and we began to identify job skills women might need. We discussed social services that are often available locally. We attempted to identify necessary qualities and characteristics of volunteers. We began to list the possible support systems the women themselves might need. We determined that everything must be done in a Christian context, and that necessitated the services of spiritually mature mentors and ongoing Bible studies for the clients.

We were committed to the development of a flexible and locally indigenous approach. Our efforts would require a needs assessment of local communities where sites were to be developed.

By the end of the meeting, we designated several steps. First, we would select a national coordinator and an advisory council. Sites for a pilot phase would be chosen. We would develop networks of churches, businesses, and volunteers. We would plan training for all volunteers, especially for the mentors, whom we felt would be critical to this approach.

It was a huge job, but every participant in that meeting left believing it was possible. Three of the state WMU directors committed to being a part of the pilot project. Bill Pinson, executive secretary of Texas Baptists, had already indicated his support, and Joy Fenner was quick to agree. Pat Lutrell became the point person for Texas, and Camille Simmons would be the local site coordinator in San Antonio. Camille gave visionary leadership and yeoman's service in the launching of the San Antonio site.

Evelyn Blount committed South Carolina to a pilot site, too; and with the assistance of Brenda Kneece of South Carolina WMU, not one but *four* sites were developed.

Evelyn Tully had already been instrumental in developing a program of assistance for women at Uptown Baptist Church in Chicago, and she was determined to take this to a new level of involvement. Other sites developed following this meeting, and you will read their stories later in this book.

We struggled with a name and statement of purpose. Several drafts were considered but at the close of the meeting on July 8, 1994, we left with these two issues unresolved. The new baby had been conceived—no name yet, later to be selected. It was an exciting beginning.

MOVING FORWARD

ON SEPTEMBER 1, 1994, Trudy Johnson was appointed to a new position at WMU, SBC. As Special Projects manager, she would assume the staff responsibility for guiding the program. She was a natural choice for leadership. With Trudy's training in social work, missionary experience, and deep commitment to the church's ministry to those in need, she had all the qualities necessary for the assignment. Since that time, Trudy has given able leadership in many areas, but primarily in this special focus.

A telephone conference of the originators from the Dallas meeting on October 26, 1994, refined plans. The name for the program, pending legal advice, would be Christian Women's Job Corps, with the thought of adding, "A Ministry of WMU."

Further discussion surrounded the subjects of structure, availability of jobs, existing models, and volunteers. The most scintillating part of the telephone conference, however, was the report time. Camille Simmons, Evelyn Tully, Frances Shaw, and Evelyn Blount recounted numerous evidences of God's going ahead to prepare the way. Each of these instances reconfirmed the rightness of the decision.

Members of the initial task force met in Birmingham on January 11–13, 1995. In addition, several site coordinators were in attendance. Each pilot state brought a report of proposed strategies and potential locations. South Carolina had formed a task force that was in the process of selecting a site and was exploring a tie with the Baptist Medical Center. Florida was considering Miami as their possible location. Illinois saw a potential in the Christian Activity Center in East St. Louis and in three areas of Chicago. Birmingham had set a date for a discussion with local civic leaders. Texas was looking at two possible sites: the Rio Grande Association, which contained two of the poorest areas in the nation; and San Antonio, a part of the ongoing Mega-Focus Cities planning of the North American Mission Board.

It was time now to begin to put flesh on the bones, to begin more specific planning. Questions surfaced in the discussion: *Does CWJC need to apply for tax-exempt status? What structures are necessary on the national, state, and local levels? What should be contained in the core curriculum? Who will become clients of CWJC? How will they be selected? What requirements will be placed on them? What roles will the project coordinator, the mentors, and other volunteers play?*

In order to explore these and other questions in depth, we formed discussion groups. The dialogue was lively, and spirits were high. At the close of the meeting, the results were like a plowed field from which rocks had been extracted; the ground dug up, furrows beginning to be formed. The land was now ready for planting. The consensus of the task force was that their work was complete. The time had come for the more permanent national body to be named and to begin working.

While the national Christian Women's Job Corps advisory council was being organized, pilot sites were encouraged to continue their local development. While some principles appeared to be general across all sites, it was our goal that each location develop a plan that uniquely fit its community. We were eager that the pilots offer a diversity of approaches, so that we could identify strategies that "worked." The

models were indeed different, with several being based in an
association, some with a local church, and one was even one
woman with one woman. However, three universals were
required:

    1. Each site would operate in a Christian context.
Leadership would be drawn from local churches,
especially from Women on Mission® groups.

    2. Each site's curriculum would include Bible study.
This was considered to be the factor that made CWJC
unique; it would therefore be essential.

    3. Each woman would be assigned a mentor, a
woman who would be a spiritual and personal guide
to walk alongside the client. Special training would
be provided for mentors. This too was considered to
be a factor unique to CWJC and a key to empowering
women to successful self-sufficiency.

While many decisions were still to be made on the national level, basic components were in place. Word began to cir-
culate among WMU groups, and general excitement developed. As reports came in from the field, inquiries multiplied
and interest grew. In response to the questions, a one-page
statement was circulated for clarification of this new initiative of WMU. Trudy Johnson created a thought-provoking
true-false test to further acquaint our membership with
CWJC, even as it was being fleshed out in the pilot sites.

NATIONAL TASK FORCE FORMED
ON OCTOBER 31, 1996, the newly formed national CWJC
National Task Force met in Birmingham, Alabama. This
national task force was made up of the following members:
Evelyn Blount, Columbia, South Carolina; C. Anne Davis,
Louisville, Kentucky; Jane Ferguson, Montgomery, Alabama;
Vickie Furr, Vestavia Hills, Alabama; Beverly Hammack,
Conyers, Georgia; Martha Hawkins, Montgomery, Alabama;
Peggy Hicks, Louisville, Kentucky; Dorothy McPhail,
Demopolis, Alabama; Bob Mills, Atlanta, Georgia (now serv-
ing in Kansas); Marlene Reed, Birmingham, Alabama;

Richard Smith, Birmingham, Alabama. Ex officio members were Dellanna O'Brien, Birmingham, Alabama and Wanda Lee, Columbus, Georgia.

Among the group were WMU leaders; experts in job programs, volunteerism, and community ministry; an attorney; a nurse; business and social work professors; and a former woman in need, now a successful businesswoman. This was a work group, comprised of those with the expertise to direct the decisions of CWJC.

We spent the first day of the October meeting listening to reports from the pilot sites. We were amazed at what God had already begun to do. The second day provided training for the site coordinators and the first formal meeting of the CWJC National Task Force.

Major issues facing the national task force included: liability at the state, national, and local levels; certification training and supervision; federal funding; evaluation; eight program elements; and relationships between state and national (WMU) entities.

The task force scheduled the first national training event for July 1997, to be held at WMU's national headquarters in Birmingham. The training program would yield national certification. A graphic—two hand-shaped, red flowers on a stem—was confirmed as the official logo of CWJC. A video was commissioned to tell the story of CWJC. The pilot evaluation was slated for March 1, 1997. The group adopted the following purpose statement: To provide a Christian context in which women in need are equipped for life and employment and to provide a missions context in which women help women. This statement brought purpose not only to the women who would be the clients but also to those Christian women who would serve as mentors and volunteers.

GOD'S TIMING IS ALWAYS PERFECT

MEANWHILE, BACK ON the CWJC sites, much was happening. The passion with which the leaders in each site claimed the purpose of CWJC and the quality of their work could never have been solicited through high salaries. God had a higher claim on their lives, and He had placed a vision in their hearts. Hundreds of volunteers came to offer their services. Even children in missions education organizations in the churches found ways to help. The success of the work of CWJC was due to the dedication and hard work of the local site core. And their reward? To understand this, you must read their stories.

One factor, however, which none of us who convened in Dallas for that first historic meeting in July 1994 could have known, proved to be God's evidence that the timing of CWJC was right. In 1997, just when the training would enable almost 200 new sites to be launched, our nation was faced with one of its most gargantuan challenges. Welfare reform required that those who had lived off checks from the government would now have to be employed. For women especially, this seemed almost an impossible task. Most of the women on welfare were single parents, responsible for their children as well as themselves. Many had no job skills, lived in areas where there were no available jobs, little or no public transportation, and few or no affordable child-care facilities. Without intervention, this feat could not be accomplished.

Government leaders recognized the necessity for the involvement of churches to train and equip people for jobs, to assist them in moving from welfare to self-sufficiency. When CWJC came to the attention of Vice-President Al Gore, he deemed it a worthy model for our nation. He invited Trudy Johnson to represent CWJC on a newly formed national Welfare to Work Coalition to Sustain Success as a charter member, giving the ministry national visibility. Today, representing CWJC, Trudy convenes with other program leaders in identifying strategies for moving people off the welfare rolls and into employment. God's timing is faultless!

But CWJC is unique, for its target is women who want more out of life than just a job. Christ offered His followers abundant life, and He allows us to be the bearers of this good news. In the next years, we will see countless women come to know Him and embrace His gift of abundant life through Christian Women's Job Corps.

2

The
Remarkable Story of
York County
Christian Women's Job Corps

THE REMARKABLE STORY OF
YORK COUNTY CHRISTIAN WOMEN'S JOB CORPS

When I was hungry, you gave me something to eat, and when I was thirsty, you gave me something to drink. When I was a stranger, you welcomed me, and when I was naked, you gave me clothes to wear. When I was sick, you took care of me, and when I was in jail, you visited me. Whenever you did it for any of my people, no matter how unimportant they seemed, you did it for me (Matt. 25: 35–36,40, CEV).

In September of 1995 a tremendous storm hit South Carolina. Residents of the state were unprepared for its impact. The storm was not covered in national headlines; no federal relief money or emergency personnel were pressed into service in the storm's aftermath. Yet the after-effects are increasingly visible. The storm's name? Christian Women's Job Corps. The target of the storm? Women in need. The aftermath? One woman ministering to one woman to change her world!

Evelyn Blount, executive director of Woman's Missionary Union auxiliary to the South Carolina Baptist Convention, volunteered for her state to pilot the CWJC concept. York Association, which includes the community of Fort Mill, was asked in September 1995 to be one of the test sites. Evelyn's enthusiasm for the new ministry of WMU was contagious.

"To me it's the single most comprehensive approach that Southern Baptists have ever had in meeting the needs of people. The program is designed to help them become self-sufficient—to have a self-sustaining lifestyle in the Christian context."

Jane's life has been permanently changed because of her involvement in Christian Women's Job Corps. Her story demonstrates the hope CWJC offers women in need. Jane gives meaning to the term mid-life crisis. Jane and her teenage daughter were living in government subsidized housing on a combined income of $80 a week. Jane earned $50 a week baby-sitting and received $30 in child support.

For eleven years, Jane was a good and faithful worker at the local mill. Standing on concrete floors took its toll on Jane and she developed lower back and leg problems. Jane's doctors told her that she would lose her ability to walk if she stayed on the job. She felt trapped. Jane continued working until she was laid off. Her health problems, lack of marketable skills, and lack of transportation made Jane unemployable.

Like all CWJC participants, Jane's mentor played a tremendous role in her move from dependency to self-sufficiency. Her mentor encouraged Jane as she set goals for her life. Two of Jane's prominent goals were for job-skill training for herself and a college education for her daughter. Jane also harbored a desire to learn to drive so that more employment opportunities would be open to her.

The remarkable story of CWJC demonstrates the hope experienced by Jane and her daughter. The daughter was given a full grant to attend college. Jane herself completed training with Vocational Rehabilitation and is managing a coin laundry within walking distance of her home. She still has dreams of learning to drive and of moving into a home of her own.

When Jane participated in a CWJC celebration at the York Baptist Association office she had the experience of a lifetime. Amid joy and tears, she held a flower given to participants and exclaimed: "No one has ever given me a rose before. I feel so special."

Everyone who is privileged to know Jane agrees that she

is special. They describe her as a natural mentor. In addition to actively promoting Christian Women's Job Corps among her family and friends, Jane plans to someday receive CWJC mentor training so that she too can help a woman break out of the poverty cycle.

"To see a woman change before your eyes, grow spiritually, get an education, stand on her own—it's like watching a flower bloom." That is how York Association CWJC site coordinator Elizabeth Ford describes what she has experienced since joining the CWJC program in November of 1996.

York Association Christian Women's Job Corps has continued to grow since Elizabeth said "yes" to the invitation to serve as project coordinator. The sparkle in her eyes, the bounce in her step, the broad smile on her face, and her vocal enthusiasm are testimony to how God has worked through Elizabeth and blessed her with a fulfilling ministry.

When South Carolina WMU asked York Association to be a pilot site, Elizabeth was serving as their volunteer Woman's Missionary Union director. She was employed full-time and enjoyed her job, as well as her WMU work. God had other plans for Elizabeth! Now a full-time Mission Service Corps volunteer through the North American Mission Board, Elizabeth shares: "I immediately realized God was ahead of me as usual, and had worked all of this out. My assignment for Mission Service Corps became Christian Women's Job Corps, and I worked at least 20 hours a week at it. Before the pilot had gone very far, we knew it would be an ongoing ministry of the area as long as there was a need. As the months passed from January to August 1996, I began to feel God leading me to do Christian Women's Job Corps full-time.

"I was spending more and more time working on the ministry, and I knew the benefits of having the opportunity to work on it full-time, but I could not see how we could afford for me to give up my salaried job. Plus I was working with women in my job, many of the same type of women, educating them in cancer prevention. I really loved what I was doing.

"God made it clear what He wanted, so my husband and I stepped out on faith and went to a one-salary household. There have been some touchy times, but God has provided and we have no regrets. We both believe in this ministry totally."

Like all state CWJC sites, South Carolina WMU serves the York Association site by identifying resources, and providing training, encouragement and support.

How did CWJC get started in South Carolina?

After committing to pilot CWJC in South Carolina, a state CWJC Task Force was organized to help develop the program and training materials. Members of the task force were selected for their expertise in areas of industry, health care, education, poverty, career counseling, grants, business, and politics. Brenda Kneece and Evelyn Blount provided leadership in developing a training notebook that introduced information about the nature of the SC project and their guidelines; resources; the key participants of client, mentor, advocate, and project coordinator; principles of mentoring; resource networking; job opportunity network; suggested implementation schedule; necessary and duplicable forms; and related background articles.

Only acknowledgment of the involvement of God in the development of CWJC can explain how so many things have been accomplished in such a short period of time. His promise to provide a hope and a future has been fulfilled in York Association!

In September 1995 York Association was asked to be a CWJC pilot site. The South Carolina CWJC Task Force met with interested persons, including then WMU director Elizabeth Ford, to overview the project. In October, York Association church members including women active in WMU joined staff members to hear the vision for the new ministry. By November a CWJC council had been selected. In December of the same year, all social service and helping agencies in the county were included in a discussion of the plans for CWJC.

In 1996, the exciting year began with Dr. C. Anne Davis training the first six mentors in January. In February, the first three clients began their CWJC journey. Public relations was the focus in March when a brochure was prepared to encourage mentors and other volunteers to consider involvement in

CWJC. In April, leaders began developing their mentor training manual and were actively recruiting mentors. Kingdom Cars, an avenue through which dealerships and people in York County donate used cars to CWJC clients, became a reality for CWJC clients in May. The summer months were a time for leaders to develop materials, conduct training for mentors, add clients, and establish quarterly celebrations. In September, Elizabeth Ford led a CWJC conference at the associational fall WMU training. A much-anticipated milestone was reached in October when the first client reached self-sufficiency. Another significant event occurred in November when Elizabeth became the first full time CWJC project coordinator.

CWJC's growth continued into 1997. As ministry to women in need grew, so did the awareness of unmet needs in the county. In February, the association formed a task force to begin a Parish Nurse Ministry. What was the purpose of this new ministry? To provide medical screening and referral services to CWJC clients. Nurses would also cultivate a network within the medical community for providing reduced cost medical services for the county's poor. The goal of developing volunteer training and education for CWJC was part of this plan. Children and youth were the focus of the associational implementation of a Big Brother/Big Sister ministry in March. April was the month a Cottage Industry program was begun. This innovative addition to the CWJC ministry was designed to help women work full-time from home. The problems of child care and transportation were creatively solved.

How does it work?

THE FOCUS OF CWJC in South Carolina is on one woman helping one woman break the cycle of poverty. Like York Association, each SC Christian Women's Job Corps site utilizes a holistic approach to meet the total needs of each woman—spiritual, physical, emotional, and educational. No woman is turned away from CWJC. Some women might be referred to another program if they need to deal with substance abuse issues or need help with reading and writing. A mentor may still be assigned to the woman to encourage her as she prepares for job skills training.

Each CWJC site keeps the needs of women in their community in mind when designing their unique program. Even across South Carolina, no two CWJC programs are identical. Nationally there is even more variation. At the heart of each program are the eight key elements of CWJC as adopted by the National Task Force (see page 00). Individualized for South Carolina, their guidelines stipulate:

• There will be a mentor for every client.
• There will be a covenant agreement with every mentor and with every client.
• The client will participate in weekly Bible study.
• Networking with the community and with other churches will be used.
• Needs assessment will be done.
• There will be a state advisory council that will continue to function and work.
• The Project Coordinators will be certified and participate in the training for their certification.
• There will be ongoing evaluation.
• Sites will be locally funded.
• There will be reports to South Carolina WMU.

A Christian mentor is assigned to every participant from the time she enters the program until she is self-sufficient. Every client's needs are assessed. Each participant signs an individualized covenant agreeing to participate in Bible study. All clients attend training classes, support groups, and meet other requirements of her individualized plan.

Counseling and assistance in the areas of employment, money management, parenting skills, and self-esteem are customized to meet the needs of the individual woman. Mentors and project coordinators access community resources through networking. Every mentor serves under a covenant that is individually developed based upon the client's needs, gifts, skills, and available time.

All women in the CWJC program make the long-term goal to become mentors when they reach self-sufficiency. Finally, state or national WMU trains all project coordinators and there is intentional ongoing evaluation of all aspects of the CWJC ministry.

The project coordinator serves as the hub for Christian Women's Job Corps as she networks and accesses resources in the community. In York Association, Elizabeth Ford draws upon the volunteer resources of many in order to meet the needs of their participants. She communicates with community organizations, churches, and city government.

"One of the first things we did when we were asked to pilot this project was to bring all the service agencies together. We've been really astounded at their response. It's like God had been working in their lives without them knowing, preparing the way for this program. So we've been able to network with them and provide the resources that we didn't have for our clients to meet their needs," Elizabeth states.

When a woman first contacts Christian Women's Job Corps, she is guided through an application process. Next the project coordinator assesses the woman's situation to determine what specific needs she has, whether physical, educational, spiritual, relational, or emotional. The new client is matched with a mentor and together they develop a covenant, which becomes a personalized plan of action. This covenant identifies what the client needs in order to gain life and job skills that can lead her to self-sufficiency. Her mentor will encourage her, guide her to resources, model positive life skills, and pray for her.

Mentors are someone the client can trust—something that many women in need have never had in their lives. There are no deadlines or time limits for the mentor-client relationship, so mentors can work with their clients as long as it takes for them to become self-sufficient. This kind of relationship offers confidence to the client. Each woman knows her mentor is committed to her for the long haul.

Elizabeth Ford describes the matching process of client to mentor. "Since I do the intake on the clients as well as the training of the mentors, I know both women fairly well by the time they need to be matched. I consider geographic location, spiritual gifts, personalities. Mostly I depend on the Holy Spirit. I begin to pray for each mentor's assignment when I receive her application. By the time she has completed the first half of her training, the Holy Spirit usually has impressed me whom to assign to her. I pray long and hard for discernment."

The mentor and client develop specific goals based on their brainstorming about what her urgent needs are. Week by week, they address those needs. A client may need to figure out how to get food for the rest of the month, how to arrange for child care, or how to deal with an abusive relationship. Normally at the beginning of the relationship, a client's needs are for her immediate life concerns. As she is able to succeed in accomplishing goals, she is able to identify other dreams and goals.

Quarterly celebrations are a critical part of the ministry of Christian Women's Job Corps. Many of these women have little joy in their lives, so they learn to celebrate. The celebration focuses on a theme and incorporates inspiration, fellowship, as well as a topic of interest for the women. These celebrations also become an avenue for entire churches to become involved. Woman's Missionary Union™ age-level organizations, such as Acteens™, Mission Friends™, Girls In Action™, and Women on Mission™ may provide decorations and refreshments, serve as hostesses, or prepare gift bags to give away at the celebrations.

THE REMARKABLE DIFFERENCE CWJC MAKES

MUCH EARLIER THAN anticipated, the CWJC National Task was able to evaluate the success of the pilot projects, like those in South Carolina and conclude that CWJC works! The difference it makes is seen in the lives of mentors and their clients. The story of the women of CWJC and God at work in their lives and this program is indeed remarkable!

CWJC made a difference in Chelsea's life. She grew up being forced to make drug pick-ups for her father who was a dealer. At a young age, Chelsea got involved with a dealer who fathered her four children. Following his arrest, Chelsea found herself a single mother living in the trailer owned by the stepfather of her boyfriend. The food stamps Chelsea received went to the stepfather who in turn decided how much she and her children should receive.

Chelsea started school in York and needed a baby-sitter but couldn't afford one. When someone first gave her a brochure about CWJC she ignored it. Not long after, someone at Social Services encouraged Chelsea to consider CWJC.

Chelsea wanted her life to be different. She wanted to change the way she acted, the way she thought about the things, the choices she made. Chelsea wanted to move away from the trailer and secure a job that would enable her to support her children. Chelsea did not want to have to rely on welfare. Without an education, she knew much stood in the way of her realizing her dreams.

What difference does CWJC make to Chelsea? Hear her as she talks about Marie, her mentor. "Some people say there's a guardian angel among us, well, she's mine. She was sent from heaven to support me. I can tell her things that nobody will ever know, that I've never told anyone, and I know it won't go any further than her."

Marie helped Chelsea find a job and supported her through difficult times when Chelsea shifted back into her old lifestyle of drinking in bars. One day, Marie's husband saw Chelsea working at a fast-food restaurant. He told her that it would really please Marie if she attended church with them. Chelsea promised to go the next Sunday, and Marie willingly volunteered to provide Chelsea and her children with a ride. Through the love and support of Marie and her family, Chelsea came to hear about Jesus Christ and understand her need to acknowledge Him as her Savior. She now plans to raise her children in a Christian home.

Chelsea is now employed full-time and working toward her next goal of better housing. Christian Women's Job Corps has made an enormous difference in her present and her future!

While the change from a dependent lifestyle to one of self-sufficiency is remarkable enough, there is more to the CWJC story! Marie's experience with Chelsea helps convey the impact of CWJC on the mentor!

By her own admission, mentoring has really stretched Marie. She views it much like parenting, as she is lovingly guiding someone away from potential dangers and mistakes. "I'm getting the benefit of learning from someone else's mistakes. Now I sit down with my six and eleven-year-olds and talk about what's right and what's wrong and living with the consequences of your actions and accepting responsibility."

When Marie was matched with Chelsea, she realized that there was no one else to give Chelsea guidance. "There was no one who cared enough to say NO. They just let her go her own way, and at 13-14 years old you don't have the experience or the background to make a lot of right choices with nobody to back you up. That's one thing I've done with her."

Marie's whole family has gotten involved with Chelsea and her children. Their family visits Chelsea at the restaurant where she works, and she takes breaks and spends time with them. After having so few healthy family relationships, Chelsea has been able to observe how Marie and her husband interact as Christian parents and loving, committed husband and wife. Drawing from their experience, Chelsea asks a lot of questions, especially about how to handle discipline problems with children.

Marie knew that involving Chelsea in church would offer her another lifestyle choice. The church family gave her a support system. No longer did Chelsea feel like she was all alone as a single mother. She even realized she had an alternative from returning to an abusive relationship with her boyfriend.

The fact that Marie and her family live in a trailer too helped Chelsea. She could see things they had in common. A noticeable difference was the love that fills Marie's home. Chelsea began trusting Marie more when she discovered Marie was telling her the truth about Jesus and that she kept her word. When Marie's friends helped transport Chelsea, she would inundate them with questions to see if Marie was telling her the truth about Jesus.

One woman to one woman, Chelsea and Marie. Both women are forever changed because of Christian Women's Job Corps! But they are not alone!

At 18, Lisa journeyed from South Carolina to San Antonio, Texas, to join 10,000 other teenaged girls at a National Acteens Convention, a missions conference sponsored by WMU. Her life was not that of a stereotypical, churchgoing teen. Lisa came from a very dysfunctional family. She left home immediately after high school graduation. While she was working, she became involved in an unhealthy relationship and became pregnant.

It was Lisa's pastor's wife, Davlyn, who first told her of Christian Women's Job Corps. Lisa describes her life at that point: "I was renting a trailer and I was basically living day-to-day; well, actually week-to-week. Struggling, you know, working a 40-hour job, I was just working, going to work and home, and going to church on Wednesday and Sunday. Just trying to live for the Lord and do the best I could trying to raise a daughter being a single parent. I was at a point in my life where I just wanted to do something different."

Lisa and Davlyn were matched as a client and mentor. Davlyn has become like a mother to Lisa and helped her grow spiritually. "It's helped me to grow tremendously, as a Christian and as a single parent. We get together weekly and do our Bible study. We have different books that we go through to study. We read our Bibles and talk about how it pertains to our daily life and how it's helping us to grow as Christians. She's my prayer partner and prays for me daily," exclaims Lisa.

A significant change in Lisa's life is her relationship with her family. Because of her spiritual growth in the Lord, this relationship has been restored. She now lives at home while she is finishing school.

Lisa completed her first year at York Tech and intends to complete her medical lab technician degree. She works a full-time job and goes to school four nights a week. She has recently obtained a computer, with the help of CWJC, which helps her with her studies. Lisa's dream is to be in the medical field. She wants to be able to work with people and help others either through nursing or through Christian Women's Job Corps.

What about Davlyn? She first heard about Christian Women's Job Corps in November 1995 at the South Carolina Baptist Convention. She felt the Lord urging her to get involved helping women outside of the church. When she returned from the convention, she received a postcard inviting her to an informational meeting about CWJC in York Association. "I was not sure that I could be a mentor because I was a pastor's wife with a full-time job. I didn't know if I could really devote enough time to Christian Women's Job

Corps to be a mentor, but I began to pray about it and the Lord did lead me to become involved."

Davlyn has seen many answers to prayer with Lisa, the woman she mentors. She relies on the prayer network in her church set up by their Women on Mission, a missions organization for adult women sponsored by WMU. They pray daily for Lisa and Davlyn. "God has been very faithful in answering those prayers for her. We've prayed about things. We've cried together. We've asked the Lord to perform miracles for her, and God has really done that."

Terry and Monieca are another woman-to-woman, client and mentor pair who answer the question, what difference does CWJC make? Terry is a 35-year-old single mother. Before Christian Women's Job Corps, "I was about to lose the home that I had. My self-esteem was real low; I was having a lot of problems, a lot of financial problems. I wasn't going to church either," shares Terry.

Through CWJC, Terry has taken parenting classes, improved her job skills, and secured a better job. She has moved into transitional housing and is working toward securing permanent housing for herself and her daughter. Just like other women in CWJC, setting goals has been a step-by-step process for Terry. Her faith has enabled her to quickly grasp the covenant relationship with her mentor, and Terry is committed to reaching her goal of self-sufficiency.

Monieca is Terry's mentor and recognizes their relationship will grow into a lasting friendship. Terry has learned that Monieca is someone she can count on for guidance. Together they study the Bible and discuss Terry's goals, what she has accomplished, and what she has yet to achieve. With Monieca's help, Terry now has health insurance and is well on her way to meeting her goals.

How did Monieca become involved in CWJC? A social worker at Pilgrim's Inn, a helping agency for single mothers, Monieca heard about Christian Women's Job Corps at church and knew she wanted to be involved. Daily she encounters women like Jane, Lisa, Chelsea, and Terry.

Monieca notes that CWJC is different from other community-based helping agencies. "Each week the requirement for our program is that you participate in a Bible study. It is a Christian program and we have an opportunity to share with our clients about Christ, help them learn about faith in Christ or grow as Christians." The spiritual encouragement Monieca gives Terry by helping her become more involved in church has helped Terry become stronger as she works to achieve her goals.

Monieca shared Davlyn's concern that she might not have enough time for mentoring a CWJC client. Monieca's employment is part-time, she has two children, and her husband is also in the ministry. "But I felt that as a church it was a great opportunity—being a church member, being a Christian—to reach out to women in our community and share Christ. I think being where God wants you to be, it's fun to help someone else and to see them progress; to see someone doing well; to be able to encourage and to make a new relationship with someone. If God wants us there, He'll provide the way, and He'll provide the time. It's been amazing to me that I have found the time to work with CWJC."

UNIQUELY YORK COUNTY

MIKE O'DELL, the missions development director for York Baptist Association, describes the transition that York County is facing as one of the fastest growing counties in South Carolina. Because of its proximity to Charlotte, North Carolina, it is a bedroom community for Charlotte. Despite the economic growth, 15 percent of the population in York County lives at or below the poverty level. Single mothers head 90 to 95 percent of families in poverty.

Despite its growth, York County is still a rural area. One great challenge is transportation. Unlike many metropolitan areas, mass transportation is available only in certain areas. Many CWJC clients face the formidable task of finding housing and reasonable transportation. Taxis are available but are very expensive. Without transportation, however, women have fewer opportunities for training and employment.

Many of the women involved in Christian Women's Job Corps are not prepared for life's crises. They may lack the training, support systems, education, or the financial base to combat problems. Suddenly women find themselves out on their own with few resources to survive above the poverty level. Even educated women may be without any family or friends to support them. Christian Women's Job Corps offers these kinds of women a place to begin again.

CWJC in each community benefits from networking with other helping agencies. York Association has found many needs can and are being met by other groups. Utilizing their services and avoiding duplication magnifies the assistance that can be given to women in need!

In Fort Mill, Bridgebuilders is an interdenominational group that builds houses for homeless women and children. They maintain the house, pay the utilities, and furnish the house. Bridgebuilders has an agreement with Christian Women's Job Corps to provide housing for their clients. By spring of 1998, they had accommodated six families.

In May 1996, the York Association CWJC began a program called Kingdom Cars. Dealerships and individuals in the community donate good, used automobiles to CWJC clients. Cars are given to women who are well on the road to self-sufficiency and who can provide routine maintenance and insurance. In the spring of 1998, one of the first women to benefit from being the recipient of a Kingdom Car transferred the title to another CWJC client. Why? The original CWJC owner was able to afford her own vehicle!

The city of Rock Hill has given Christian Women's Job Corps two lots on which to build houses. CWJC hopes to partner with Habitat for Humanity and Brotherhood Builders, two organizations dedicated to building affordable housing for low-income families, to build houses on their lots.

There are many other agencies that partner with Christian Women's Job Corps in York Association. There are US government agencies such as the Department of Social Services, Home Health Social Services, WIC (Women, Infant, and Children) food supplement program, Job Training Placement Act, and the Government Housing Authority. There are state agencies such as the Mental Health Department, South Carolina Employment Security Commission, and York Technical College. Community agencies Christian Women's Job Corps networks with are Babynet (which works with special needs children), Keystone (a substance abuse program), the City of Rock Hill housing authority, Sister Help (a service for abused women), school systems, adult education programs, Habitat for Humanity, and evangelical churches.

THE ROLE OF PRAYER

HELEN IS A 36-year-old mother of three and grandmother of one. Unlike most York CWJC clients, she is married. Helen's husband is disabled. Family debts were rising and the family was sinking fast. However, shortly after becoming involved in CWJC, Helen caught something life changing: hope! Not long after this book goes to print, Helen will graduate from high school along with her two daughters. She has a new, better-paying job with benefits, and has paid off two outstanding debts by learning to live within her family budget.

Helen's hope has impacted her family! Her husband has lost the 30 pounds necessary to be placed on an organ donor list for a new kidney. Helen admits that none of the changes in her life have come easily. She openly testifies to the power of answered prayer!

Site coordinator Elizabeth Ford shares the vital role prayer plays in her life. "My church commissioned me as a Mission Service Corps volunteer after I had my assignment, so my church covenanted with me to pray faithfully, volunteer, and help provide resources. The director of missions, Ned Duncan, is a wonderful part of my spiritual support; also Mike O'Dell, our church and community ministries staff person. My husband and three sons have proven to be some of my strongest support. With these men praying for me, things happen! Christian Women's Job Corps council and mentors are also good means of support."

HOPE FOR THE FUTURE

IT WAS JUST February 1996 when York Association began CWJC with three clients. By October of that same year the first client had achieved self-sufficiency! Remarkably, CWJC is changing the lives of women in need in South Carolina!

Elizabeth Ford has a big vision for Christian Women's Job Corps in the York Association. She recognizes the need to have at least 100 mentors working with women. She dreams of the Cottage Industry going full force, enabling women to work from home, eliminating the need for child care and transportation. Elizabeth also plans for a sewing class in which the CWJC women can make their own clothing. Her vision includes CWJC establishing a day care and a credit union. She hopes to see multiple transitional houses built in her community. But Elizabeth's vision extends beyond York Association and even beyond South Carolina as she dreams of a network of Christian Women's Job Corps ministries across the United States.

As Elizabeth reflects on the York Association pilot project she says: "God gets all the credit for anything that has been done here. I have been blessed beyond belief. Now some days all I do is deal with one crisis, one after another. And I think, oh, make this go away, make it all better. I deal with a lot of hurt; some of the women are coming from unbelievable hurt in their lives. And so as I look back over the year, I should have fallen by the way long ago and fallen apart. That I didn't is quite a testimony to me of God's faithfulness and how He has enabled me to do this."

Evelyn Blount, executive director for South Carolina WMU, believes that Christian Women's Job Corps is the wave of the future. The reason she initially became involved in WMU was its ministering-witnessing concept. "The more things we do like Christian Women's Job Corps, the bigger image we're going to have as far as being the organization that's on the cutting edge, that is willing to risk, that is willing to give time in order to help people be Christian. It has the potential of revolutionizing who we are as Woman's Missionary Union. People are more interested in hands-on study, and this is the way that they can become involved."

A former client recently spoke at a statewide meeting. Martha shared how difficult it had been for her to make the call to Christian Women's Job Corps and ask for help. She had been a financially independent, steady worker. While at home with a newborn, she fell behind in her bills and was forced to move out of her apartment and into the home of a friend. Her eyes sparkled and her smile was radiant as she shared what CWJC has meant to her. Martha is now employed and close to self-sufficiency. She dreams of buying a home. But that isn't her only dream! This former client looks forward to becoming a CWJC mentor. How remarkable indeed!

I know Him

I will hold on.

I will never let go.

I swim across the ocean to reach my goal.

I may get a little weak along the way.

And I don't care what people may say.

The future of my life is about to unfold.

My Strength (Jesus), He cares for my soul.

He's the only One Who keeps encouraging me –

to hold my head up and be all that I can be.

I love You, Lord, and I thank You for everything.

To some I am a nobody, but to You I am fame.

Bobbie Ann
York County CWJC client

3

*The
Remarkable Story of
San Antonio
Christian Women's Job Corps*

THE REMARKABLE STORY OF
SAN ANTONIO CHRISTIAN WOMEN'S JOB CORPS

*"For I know the plans I have for you, says the Lord, plans
for welfare and not for evil, to give you a future and a hope.
Then you will call upon me and come and pray to me, and I
will hear you. You will seek me and find me; when you seek
me with all your heart. I will be found by you, says the Lord,
and I will restore your fortunes" (Jer. 29:11–14 CEV).*

THE GYM OF Park Hills Baptist Church was set for the graduation ceremony. Chairs were grouped in a semicircle, plants
placed around a lattice screen, brochures and newsletters lay
on a table ready to be picked up, and refreshments waited at
the side of the room. There was anticipation in the air for the
celebration to begin. Families, teachers, volunteers, minis-
ters, and Christian Women's Job Corps℠ class members sat
patiently waiting. The San Antonio CWJC℠ leadership team
scurried around making sure everything was in place for the
celebration. It is important for all—class members (referred
to as clients by some sites), mentors, families, and the leadership team to commemorate completion of the each ten-
week Christian Women's Job Corps course. For everyone the
ceremony marks their accomplishments and acknowledges
their next future plans and dreams.

Typical of other graduations, this ceremony opened with

class members reading a poem together. The topic for the fifth class was What Is A Winner? Each woman described what it meant to her to be a winner. At the conclusion, they asked in unison, "What is a winner?" One-by-one students' named were called. "A winner is Shawna, Debbie, Judy, Lisa, Heather, and Amber. A winner can be someone like you." Then instructors presented a challenge to class members ready to begin their job search. Linda Gwathmey, Christian Women's Job Corps project coordinator, presented certificates of completion for class members. In conclusion one of the class members, sang a tribute that she wrote to her class entitled "So Positive." The touching lyrics identified each woman's unique personality and spoke of the special bond they shared. Many in attendance wept as they realized how God had brought each of the class members to this point of accomplishment.

Anyone who mingled with those in attendance at the reception met Christian Women's Job Corps leadership team members, mentors, class members, and instructors. Visible were smiles, tears, and hugs exchanged as sisters shared their joy with one another. The image of hope was surely imprinted by all that participated; the kind of hope that comes from Christians encouraging one another to be all that God hopes they will be.

San Antonio is home to many women in need. Those who have made the transition from dependency to self-sufficiency have a remarkable story.

Elaine fled from her violent husband to a women's shelter. Her dreams were of a better life for her two preschoolers. Elaine had goals and was aware of some of the changes needed in her life. When she began her CWJC course, Elaine knew her English needed improvement. She knew she needed to learn to dress appropriately. She knew she wanted to learn how to use a computer and develop marketable job skills.

Elaine was able to move into transitional housing and utilize food stamps to feed her family. She has filed for child support from her husband. Listen to Elaine: "My dream is to work with young children. I love to see where children grow. My heart is with children. When I was a child, I had a hard time with my feelings. I want to be there for children. It's a hard world without any guidance."

Amber is an attractive young woman who met Elaine at the women's shelter. Together they took the ten-week Christian Women's Job Corps course, and are now great friends. Amber is separated from her son, who lives in New Jersey, but her 12-year-old daughter lives with her. When she came to the shelter, Amber feared for her life. She struggles with clinical depression because of the abuse she endured, but she is taking positive steps to rise above her difficulties.

Amber shared a success story about taking a test in the Christian Women's Job Corps newsletter. "At first, I was a little nervous, but when I opened the book to the first test (vocabulary) I gasped! To my surprise everything there I had learned in Christian Women's Job Corps. I was so excited. I finished the test early and had time to double-check it. The reading test was even better. Math was the same. I never knew what we were doing in class would benefit me with that test. It was great! The class strengthened me academically and psychologically. Eight weeks before, I had a phobia about taking any kind of test. My anxiety would absolutely soar, and I was always defeated. No more!" Amber hopes to work in communications someday at a radio station.

The ministry of Christian Women's Job Corps in San Antonio is guided by three specific goals. The first is to make quality job training accessible for each client. Second is to assist each woman in evaluating her personal life skills and development and to provide an intentionally supportive environment over a period of two years. The third goal is to provide services within a Christian context.

HOW DID CWJC GET STARTED IN SAN ANTONIO?

THE SAN ANTONIO CWJC was designed as an association, or consortium of church, model. Churches within a commonly defined geographic area known as the San Antonio Baptist Association (SABA) pooled their resources of time, financial resources, and volunteers using their spiritual gifts, talents, and abilities to begin one of the first CWJC pilot projects.

SABA, in conjunction with other community ministry agencies such as Buckner Benevolences, had an established presence in Victoria Courts. The ministry of two-year missionary Amy Boyer, assigned to Victoria Courts, increased the visibility and credibility of the association. From the beginning, this large government housing project seemed the ideal target for the ministry of CWJC.

Christian women leaders in San Antonio began to respond to God's prompting to reach out to women in need. These women brought spiritual gifts of administration, hospitality, mercy, and encouragement. They came from backgrounds of law, medicine, career missions, business administration, social work, and counseling. These women understood that recent welfare reform changes compelled them with God's love to respond effectively and efficiently with a holistic approach to women on welfare.

Financial and spiritual assistance through the WMU Vision Fund, Mary Hill Davis State Missions Offering, Buckner Benevolences, and local WMU organizations enabled Christian Women's Job Corps in San Antonio to secure supplies, prepare manuals, hire one staff member, and set up a ten-week curriculum.

Camille Simmons, missions minister of San Antonio Baptist Association and interim supervisor of the Christian Women's Job Corps leadership team, describes her role in how Christian Women's Job Corps evolved on a national and associational level.

"In the summer of 1994, Dr. Lee, director of missions for San Antonio Baptist Association, told me about WMU pursuing a program of women helping women with job skills. He asked me to represent the association at a meeting in Dallas with other state, associational, and national missions leaders. During this meeting, I kept on thinking, Wouldn't it be wonderful if Doris could have this?

"Doris was a young, divorced mother of four whom I had known for several years. She came to our church for some assistance, and my husband led her to the Lord. I saw that she had a hunger to grow in the Lord. I saw what potential this young woman has! So as I sat in that meeting, Doris was in my thoughts. I knew that I couldn't do it alone. I didn't know at the time how to network. I knew she needed people to advocate for her, someone to be there to help her with her self-esteem. So I got really excited when I went to that meeting, and I started writing it all down as we dreamed and prayed about God's direction and will.

"In August 1994, San Antonio Baptist Association asked to be a pilot site for Christian Women's Job Corps, and we requested seed money from WMU to help us get started. I began praying for someone to help. In January 1995, God sent me someone who was an ideal person, Meg Cooper. We took the next 18 months to develop the concept of Christian Women's Job Corps for San Antonio. We met with Women on Mission groups all over the city and began to prioritize needs.

"Once we had the concept developed, we began to develop the program and the mentor training. We had a very strong conviction that this was a deeply Christian ministry, and we did not want to lose that distinctive."

How does it work?

EACH CHRISTIAN WOMEN'S JOB CORPS develops its own mission and goals. These frame what direction the ministry takes and how it is accomplished. The mission of Christian Women's Job Corps of San Antonio is compelled by beliefs that:

1. for many women in poverty an attitude of hopelessness in exiting the poverty cycle is based on real barriers that prevent them from accessing employment networks;

2. churches have a responsibility to serve the community in which they are located;

3. Christians are commissioned to reach out to others in Christ's name.

Thus, Christian Women's Job Corps in San Antonio seeks to systematically link individuals living in poverty with persons who care about them and who will help them prepare for, secure, and maintain employment, and move toward self-support. The ministry seeks to convey to each of its program participants the joy of living in a personal relationship with God through Christ. It also strives to include encouragement for each woman to participate in a faith community of her choice.

The CWJC leadership team identified four processes that can help a woman achieve permanent transition from welfare to work: career counseling, access to training opportunities, employer involvement, and systemic change. Each of these is grounded in a Christian perspective, as Christian Women's Job Corps staff, mentors, and volunteers model the grace and love of Jesus Christ. Marcia Fitzsimmons, volunteer coordinator, describes this grace: "I was humbled to see women in these circumstances. I was brought up in a single-parent family. It's only by God's grace that I was not in that shelter. It's really inspiring to know that I can be used, through an encouraging word, a smile, a song, and through my family. We all leave here different—staff, volunteers, everyone."

God's hand in bringing the right people at the right time was also evident with the involvement of Linda Gwathmey. Linda, a friend of Meg, was in the first group Texas A&M University trained to use their Project Forward Curriculum. This ten-week curriculum includes these units: Career, Communication, Community, Culture, Empowerment, Family and Child care, Health and Nutrition, Language and Math Literacy, Money Matters, Personal Discovery, and School and Education. As a licensed counselor with experience in teaching, counseling, and ministry, Linda was well-suited to become the project coordinator of Christian Women's Job Corps. Bible study was added to this ideal curriculum and San Antonio's CWJC had their course material.

The first class of Christian Women's Job Corps was held in the spring of 1996 and three women completed the program. In the second class, ten women completed the job-training course, six from the Salvation Army women's shelter and four from Baptist churches in the area. Christian Women's Job Corps in San Antonio completed three 10-week courses in 1996 and 1997 averaging 10 students each session.

THE REMARKABLE DIFFERENCE CWJC MAKES

CAMILLE'S RELATIONSHIP with Doris answers this question. "It became a helping situation. She would help me and I would help her. It's been a reciprocal thing. Once I told Doris, 'you've got what it takes to go to college.' Three weeks later, she got the courage up to say, 'Camille, you're the only person in my life who's told me that I can do anything like that!'

"Doris started the first class, but after five weeks she

dropped out; then she quit going to church. So I began praying for her. We kept on meeting, and one day, she said, 'You
know, I'm just acting like a rebellious teenage daughter.' It
was almost like saying, 'Don't give up on me.' So I said,
'You're stuck with me. You're not going to get rid of me and
I'm going to see you through this.' I kept on praying, but I
didn't want to push her too hard.

"After several months, I could tell she was feeling better,
so I talked to her again about starting the class in April. Doris
is like a butterfly coming out of cocoon. Yes, she's still shy,
but I hear the confidence in her voice.

"Now to hear her say at graduation that she wants that
telephone number to the Baptist Health Education
Institute...I know she's well on her way to getting into the
training course, and will be guaranteed a job by December."

Star was homeless, living in a women's shelter, and at
first she thought Christian Women's Job Corps would give her
a chance to get out of the shelter for five hours a day. It did-
n't take long for Star to realize that she was going to learn
about typing, computers, and how to find a job. During her
Christian Women's Job Corps experience, she fought for her
Social Security, found a place to live, and became a Christian
along with her husband. Forbidden by doctors' order to
work, Star is now a CWJC volunteer.

Star learned through Christian Women's Job Corps that, "I
can be a strong person even when I am down and out. Also I
can do whatever I put my mind to. While taking this class, I
decided to try for my GED, which I had failed on two other tries
in other states. My classmates and Linda encouraged me to
study. Two classmates came up with the money for the test. I
passed with flying colors. They helped me to believe in myself."
Friendship gave Star the encouragement she needed.

Through Christian Women's Job Corps Marcia has overcome many obstacles. She has paid off debts; completed the
CWJC course; kept a stable income; and balanced counseling,
working with Child Protective Services, and lawyer's court.
Her long-term goals are "to have a home, to have a good
environment for my children, to have a business of my own,
to help others better their environment for their children, so
it encourages the child to respect God's foundation so their

children can run and play and feel free and safety in their own neighborhood."

What difference does CWJC make? A remarkable one! Hear it in these letters written by former students written to women entering the San Antonio Christian Women's Job Corps:

"I hope that you will enjoy this class as much as I have. The teachers are just great and you cannot help but love them. They have patience and understanding to give to all. The love of God is felt from every one of them. When you finish this course, I hope that you will feel as I do—renewed in the spirit and more motivated than ever before. I know that you can do it if I can. With God all things are possible. Just look to Him. Here is wishing each and every one of you the best."

"This program has revived my life. Now I can do anything. I'm 45 years old. It's never too late to learn. I feel confident about myself now. One of the wisest things I've ever done was to enroll in this class. Don't quit or give up. Just try your best. God bless."

The stories of the no longer forgotten women struggling to sustain self-sufficiency are remarkable! So are the women who volunteer to be their mentors! In San Antonio, each mentor completes a 15-hour course that addresses issues such as self-awareness, relationships skills, goal setting, learning styles, literacy training, workplace skills, health and safety issues, parenting and family needs, and spiritual encouragement.

This basic training underscores the necessity of a vibrant, growing relationship with Jesus Christ. Mentor Vicki Walton describes what it means to be a mentor: "First, it means you have to become humble and rid yourself of pride. Being a mentor is a servant job; you are to serve another person. You must be in right relationship with Christ and daily seek His face; know that you are to show His love to another person you have just met and don't really know at all; give of yourself in time and through God's instruction. To be a mentor means to look deep inside and make sure nothing is there that would hinder your testimony to this person. A mentor is someone to pray for another and encourage someone."

The words of the students, mentors, and leadership team capture the essence of what Christian Women's Job Corps in San Antonio is doing. They testify to the power of God's mercy and wisdom as He draws women to service among the poor. They confirm that if we are willing to listen and follow His call, He will provide the resources for us—whatever we need!

UNIQUELY SAN ANTONIO

SAN ANTONIO'S HIGH growth rate is matched, sadly, by an increase in poverty. In the city there are also 100,000 adults with less than a high school education. Population census figures indicate that 35 percent of adults in San Antonio are illiterate. Reading is a skill that many take for granted, but research shows that a mother's literacy level is the greatest predictor of a child's future academic success. San Antonio's diversity is another contributor to the challenge of helping women break the cycle of poverty. Hispanics (55 percent) and African Americans (7 percent) comprise the majority of the city's population. These elements contribute to the challenges that woman on welfare face.

Referrals and word of mouth are the two primary ways a woman hears about Christian Women's Job Corps. Initially, an interested woman fills out an application and then is interviewed by someone on the Christian Women's Job Corps leadership team. Information is gleaned from that conversation that enables leaders to determine if the woman is ready for the ten-week course of job training. This is phase one.

If a woman enters and completes the course, she moves into phase two: work placement. In phase three the student is matched with her mentor as her support system is developed. Each mentor provides support and encouragement for the women as they begin the job application process. They study the Bible and pray together. This provides ongoing and sustained support for the student as she moves from dependency to self-sufficiency, from welfare to work.

Christian Women's Job Corps of San Antonio has several groups of people that influence their ministry. Their governing board makes administrative decisions and meets once a month. The Christian Women's Job Corps advisory board meets once a quarter and makes suggestions to the governing board and leadership team. Members of the advisory board also help with fund-raising. The Christian Women's Job Corps leadership team conducts the ongoing work in San Antonio. They meet weekly to discuss current issues, problems, and victories. The meetings offer the team a chance to regularly reflect on how God is responding with resources to the many challenges that come along.

San Antonio's CWJC shares a joint partnership with Woman's Missionary Union of San Antonio Baptist Association and Buckner Benevolences. Many Women on Mission organizations in local churches provide financial assistance for bus fare, child care, or lunches. Buckner Benevolences offers counseling to students on a sliding scale as needed. Patti Treadway, formerly associational WMU director for SABA, was instrumental in networking resources within San Antonio for CWJC. She says, "This is a chance for women in Sunday School organizations and Women on Mission to put feet to what they're doing. We'll take $7.50 for one woman's bus fare, or coffee filters, or food, or travel sizes of shampoo. The women who stay in the shelter don't have room for large bottles of shampoo. Whatever people bring in, we find a way to use. We keep handing out Bibles to the students. They take them back with them to the shelters and teach children in the shelters. We can always use more Bibles."

Christian Women's Job Corps could not serve students without the support of many other community agencies. Networking with the Salvation Army Women's Shelters has resulted in caseworkers referring many to CWJC. Southwest Winners and Project Quest are brokers who allocated job training funds to women they have tested and screened. Southern Baptist Hunger Relief funds provided food for students attending classes. Master File, a Baptist network, utilizes tracking of persons and families receiving donations. San Antonio Baptist Association provides Bibles for the students. Buckner Baptist Benevolences provides computers. Local Sunday School classes donate money for child care and bus tickets. And the Mary Hill Davis State Missions Offering provides operating funds and help with training.

Many students of CWJC live in a world with little security and peace. In their classroom they discover a haven, a place to feel safe. Many students comment that they felt safe and secure in their beautiful host church. Students talk of the sense of calm that comes over them when they arrive in the classroom after a chaotic wake up in a shelter, or a ride on the bus. This is a place where they can find "a peace that passes all understanding."

The following summaries of the stories of San Antonio students are eye-opening. While the women described are clients of the San Antonio CWJC, their stories are not unique to that city. That reality should serve as a wake-up call to all who are not in need to reach out to those who are! H e a r San Antonio site coordinator Linda Gwathmey as she summarizes the students' stories: "As the students share more of their stories, they often disclose a variety of hurts. They hurt physically because of chronic health problems, accidents, or abuse. They lack adequate nutrition and health care. They need eye care, glasses, and dental work. They hurt emotionally. They lack hope. They suffer depression. They need counseling. They have unresolved issues to address. They have been abandoned and mistreated in many ways. Many were abused as children. There is a high incidence of rape among these women. Many have lost custody of their children because they were unable to provide for them. They have low self-esteem and distorted self-concepts. They crave love and affirmation. Our students hunger spiritually."

PEOPLE WHO MAKE A DIFFERENCE

THE SAN ANTONIO CWJC has several groups of people who influence their ministry. Among these are their governing board that meets monthly; the advisory board that meets quarterly; and the leadership team whose weekly meetings address current issues, problems, and victories. Vital to the ongoing ministry of CWJC are leadership team members Linda, Charlene, Kay, TJ, and Vickie.

Linda Gwathmey, program coordinator, is also mother, teacher, licensed counselor, social worker, and minister. Her training and experience have provided her with a rich background for this unique ministry. "As I was drawn into

Christian Women's Job Corps, I slowly realized that I was in the right place at the right time. I was using all of my training and life experience and was daily being stretched by the demands of ministry. I am often weary and tired from the efforts, but I often feel a sense of peace about where I am and what I am doing—a real sense of resting in Jesus. I see that in God's ecology, nothing of our experience is wasted. This job training program gives women a sense of hope, that their futures can be different from their pasts, that this is a safe place. They blossom and grow and experience relationships that are not toxic or unhealthy."

"I'm learning that God does provide so well for His work," proclaims coordinator of services to students and mentors Kay Nolan. "About myself, I'm learning how little I understand the problems and extreme difficulties in the lives of those women who live in poverty. I've learned how strong and courageous they are."

CWJC business administrator TJ Williams is Linda's sister. "God gave me the gift of hospitality, and my mother taught me how to use it. I am able to help people feel at home and comfortable. Many of our students are fearful and distrusting of everyone. God gives me the words and ideas that help them know how much we love them."

THE ROLE OF PRAYER

YVETTE AND HER young daughter, Kimberly, live in a Victoria Courts apartments. Daily, Yvette looks beyond the hopelessness that can breed in public housing, beyond graffiti-littered walls, gangs, and unsupervised children. She chooses not to talk to her neighbors and keeps Kimberly inside. Yvette knows her daughter would like to go outside and play, but she fears Kimberly could be struck by a stray bullet.

Yvette was the first member of her family to need public assistance. Plunged into poverty when her daughter was born, Yvette prays she can be somebody self-sufficient for her daughter. Being dependent embarrasses her. Yvette prays she can realize her dream of a job in real estate and a more enriched environment for Kimberly.

Libby wanted a place to call her own. While living with

her sister, Libby asked Vicki, her mentor, to pray with her about this desire. God answered and Libby now has a home of her own. When Libby's father was hospitalized, she again asked Vicki to pray with her and this time with her family, as well. Talking to God and listening to Him makes a difference in all lives touched by CWJC.

CWJC of San Antonio would be ineffective without the prayer support received from local churches, Women on Mission groups, and their associational WMU leadership team. The ministry requires so much time, energy, emotional support, and spiritual compassion that those involved do so in response to their calling from the Father. It is remarkable to recognize how God has brought the staff, mentors, and other volunteers together to minister through Christian Women's Job Corps.

HOPE FOR THE FUTURE

CHRISTIAN WOMEN'S JOB CORPS of San Antonio faces many challenges surrounding their ministry to women in poverty. The leadership team has identified how critical it is to establish ongoing sources of funding for existing ministries, acquire new staff, and develop new sites. CWJC leaders also acknowledge that recruiting and training additional leaders is a vital key to assuring there are enough people to serve in times of crises. This addresses a concern that leaders could burn out from the demands placed upon them. Christian Women's Job Corps leaders are learning how to measure and report the impact of Christian Women's Job Corps in women's lives. Finally, leaders recognize they must stay ahead of the wave of women who have such great needs.

The capable, committed leadership team has dreams that match these challenges. They dream of reliable funding sources and long for multiple Christian Women's Job Corps sites. Leaders also have a vision for staying true to the mission of Christian Women's Job Corps as growth occurs, accurately documenting all that is happening and involving more Hispanic and African-American churches and volunteers.

Christian Women's Job Corps in San Antonio is considering new site starts in other parts of their city. The great interest and support they have received from city government leaders about this ministry project encourage leaders. Ensuring that Christian Women's Job Corps graduates are able to move into the workforce and become reliable workers is indeed hope for the future.

Imagine a city of former women in need sustaining successful employment and leading lives that include giving back to CWJC. Imagine employers preferring to hire CWJC graduates. Imagine the future of CWJC in San Antonio.

When We Started We Said . . .
We can't understand . . . we did.
We can't read this . . . we did.
We can't write this . . . we did.
We can't do this ourselves . . . we did.
We won't be successful . . . we are.
It won't last . . . it has.

Thank You
Christian Women's Job Corps.

With our prayers
The Second Graduating Class of 1996

4

....

*The
Remarkable Story of
Bismarck
Christian Women's Job Corps*

THE REMARKABLE STORY OF THE
BISMARCK CHRISTIAN WOMEN'S JOB CORPS

"If you are tired from carrying heavy burdens, come to me and I will give you rest. Take the yoke I give you. Put it on your shoulders and learn from me. I am gentle and humble, and you will find rest. This yoke is easy to bear, and this burden is light" (Matt. 11: 28–30 CEV).

ANYONE WITH THE abilities or resources to meet a need is called to minister. In North Dakota's capital city, needs are being met through Christian Women's Job Corps^{SM}! Mary is one example of the impact this ministry of Woman's Missionary Union can have on an individual.

Mary was born on the Belcourt Indian Reservation in North Dakota. At an early age she was separated form her six brothers and two sisters when Social Services removed the children from their home. Most of Mary's childhood was spent living at the Federal Indian School, Wahepton, South Dakota.

Mary grew, married, and became the mother of six children. She suffered through the loss of three. Mary made the decision to move to Sisseton, South Dakota, to help her son Billie, who has heart problems, care for his children. While living in Sisseton, Mary began to attend church. At the same time home missionaries Dorothy and Raymond Longie were

serving on the Sisseton reservation. Pastor Ray was instrumental in helping Mary come to know the Lord as her Savior.
Mary became very special to the Longies. And in God's
remarkable plan, the relationship would not end when
Dorothy and Ray moved to Bismarck.

Some time later, Mary had a heart attack and moved to
Bismarck to live with her brother. It was her brother that let
the Longies know when Mary arrived in town. As the friendship was renewed between these three, Dorothy recognized
that CWJC℠ could offer the support and encouragement
Mary needed to build a successful life in Bismarck.

Being a Christian Women's Job Corps participant
changed Mary's life! Clothing donated from Women on
Mission groups and other needed assistance met her basic
needs. Growing as a Christian helped Mary become a strong
witness for the Lord. Dorothy describes Mary this way: "Her
life radiates the love of Christ and her appreciation for all He
has done for her. Mary signed up with Green Thumb
Employment and Training, and at age 62 she started her first
job ever. She is now employed by an agency, located in the
same building as the CWJC center, that provides costumes
and props for civic activities.

How did CWJC get started in Bismarck?

This is Dorothy's testimony of how it all began: "My husband and I have been missionaries for many years. We were
both born and raised in North Dakota. He is a Sioux Indian
who served on several Sioux reservations in South and North
Dakota. When we first retired, we spent three years in Fargo,
North Dakota, to be near our daughter. Then we moved to
Bismarck, and we asked the Lord if we could start one more
mission and a work with seniors. I was state volunteer coordinator and shared our desire with Dewey Hickey, then our
Dakota Southern Baptist Fellowships state director. He
replied, 'Find yourself a building.'"

The state fellowship underwrote the expenses for Dorothy
and Raymond to attend a national volunteer celebration in
Texas. Joyce Nixon, a friend from Oakwood Baptist Church,
Chattanooga, Tennessee, had heard about Christian Women's
Job Corps. Joyce directed Dorothy to get information from

the WMU in Dallas while she was in Texas. "Joyce was so sure that I needed to know about Christian Women's Job Corps that she drove to Texas to be sure that I met Trudy Johnson from WMU, SBC, remembers Dorothy. That August she met Trudy Johnson, and after discussing CWJC and Dorothy's plans, Bismarck became one of the pilot sites for CWJC.

Dorothy began networking with community agencies related to job training and placement. She asked each agency if it could provide someone in leadership to work with the Christian Women's Job Corps project. Excitedly Dorothy proclaims: "Every person from the agencies was a born-again believer!" Dorothy began holding morning prayer meetings to ask God for a building and operating finances. By faith a place was located in April 1996. The initial lease was for 30 days. The Dakotas Southern Baptist Fellowship agreed to pay two months' rent.

A $5,000 grant from the North American Mission Board was awarded to the Dakotas for July–December 1996. A $10,000 grant was awarded for 1997. This paid the rent for the center. How proud Dorothy was to tell community agencies that the Southern Baptist Convention was very missions-minded and had a unique system of supporting missions through the Cooperative Program.

Self-respect, self-sufficiency, and hope are the goals of the Bismarck CWJC program. Their objectives reflect those goals: to build healthy self-esteem for women; to challenge women to define life goals; to encourage women to move toward those goals by developing life skills; to offer women opportunities to hear and respond to the gospel; to render emotional and spiritual support through a mentoring program; to furnish job training that will prepare women for the job market; to identify potential employers; and to extend opportunities for each woman to give back to CWJC.

How does it work?

WHEN A POTENTIAL participant comes to CWJC, she fills out an application and a legal and medical release. Dorothy then assesses the applicant's needs. Each participant is assigned a mentoring team. Dorothy serves as the first mentor and regularly with each woman, sometimes daily. This is what Dorothy calls the "high-maintenance stage" as she works with the participant to set and meet goals.

The second mentor for a participant comes from a middle-class family. This gives the participant an opportunity to experience what is often a lifestyle different from her own. Many women in poverty do not realize that their lives can be different.

The third mentor is related to the profession in which the participant will be working. This person helps form the bridge for the participant as she moves into the professional world.

Students may attend training in the morning or in the afternoon. During the morning, Bible studies and one-on-one share time is included. Six students at a time attend daily or at least several times a week. In addition to computer training, participants work with mentors on life skills and job training.

THE REMARKABLE DIFFERENCE CWJC MAKES

THE MENTOR/MENTEE relationship is vital to the success of Bismarck's Christian Women's Job Corps. Dorothy's experiences through the years have given her insight into how to lovingly guide women. She keeps a journal with one of her CWJC mentees, Vicki. Together they write to one another about what they feel and think.

From Dorothy to Vicki: "Over the time that you were here I have asked the Lord to give me knowledge, spiritual understanding, and wisdom. I learned the only way I could be used to work with single mothers was praying, 'Lord let Your spirit work through me.' I have mentored many young people in the last 47 years and found these truths were available to me. When you came to me, I covenanted with the Lord to be your spiritual friend and mentor. I asked the Lord to give me knowledge and spiritual understanding.

"As I was praying yesterday and asking the Lord for guidance, I felt my doubts about some of the things we talked about. They needed to be cleared before we signed a covenant. I need to be sure you understand the responsibility of it. I am not sure that you really understand that your presence here involves a true commitment to the Lord, your church, and pastor, and not to me as an individual."

Vicki shares her response, "Wow, I don't understand what that was all about. I am feeling really confused and sad that Dorothy doesn't trust me for some reason. I have never been as honest and straightforward before. I guess my feelings are really hurt. I feel like too much is expected of me at this point in time."

The participants of Christian Women's Job Corps in Bismarck are senior adults, single mothers with children, women with disabilities, college graduates, abused women, women recovering from substance abuse, and women in need of someone to help them not just survive, but thrive. Nancy is one of the Christian Women's Job Corps participants. She is a Christian from one of the Bismarck area churches. Nancy is disabled and dependent on a motorized scooter. Her blind husband is in a nursing home. However, Nancy's strong faith in the Lord and determination has enabled her to seek and find employment. She is employed as a motel housekeeper. She maneuvers cleaning up to 35 rooms a day on her scooter. Her employer, church, and local Christian Women's Job Corps have been a great source of support for Nancy and her husband.

Anna is a senior adult, a Southern Baptist church member, and participant of Christian Women's Job Corps and Green Thumb Employment. Her financial burden was so overwhelming that she would sit with Dorothy and cry. Anna was encouraged to update her skills, but her fear of using a computer prevented her from trying. Dorothy shares, "For several weeks, we had groups surrounding her with prayer. She attended a computer course through Green Thumb and lost her fear of the computer. However, we could not find her a job that matched her job skills and allowed for her physical disabilities. Anna still went out and volunteered at a local community service agency that housed and fed the poor. Through a casual conversation with the manager, she mentioned that she was looking for work. She is now employed at that agency as a receptionist and operates a computer."

Vicki was one of the first participants in Bismarck's CWJC. A single mother of three preschool children, she was dependent on Aid to Families with Dependent Children. Now Vicki fulfills her requirement for volunteer hours by serving at Bismarck's Christian Women's Job Corps center. Dorothy wanted to put her on the payroll and began praying about how to provide for Vicki.

Vicki has a college associates degree in criminal justice and attended Northwestern Bible College. She wants to complete her education so she can be self-sufficient. She wants to provide for her children so they will have opportunities in the future. Vicki has reenrolled in college. She expresses a desire to be a better mother and Christian. On a professional level, Vicki wants to develop her administrative and communication skills so she can make a difference in other people's lives.

In her journal, Vicki describes some of her struggles. "Today we worked on a covenant together. There are five things in my life that are causing me an enormous amount of stress. Part of our plan is to work me out of this burden. There are assertiveness problems with my family, certain friends, my sister, and two men that are a part of my life. There are issues of anger and the reactions I am receiving from my children."

It is encouraging for Vicki to know that there is someone like her mentor whom she can count on as she makes lifestyle changes. The changes are challenging and require a step-by-step plan. Vicki struggles with the challenges daily—changing attitudes, parenting adjustments, dealing with procrastination, and eliminating harmful relationships and habits. Here are some of her thoughts as she juggles family, school, and work.

"Today I'm feeling totally overwhelmed because of school. I have caused myself some self-inflicted stress by my art of procrastination. I have fallen incredibly behind in my statistics class and now tonight there is a test. I was going to make up a sob story for the teacher and see if he would have any compassion on me. Then I decided that I would go to him and tell him the truth because it's more of a sob story than anything I could ever make up. But now I have decided that I'm not going to go to him at all. I'm not going to ask for any special favors. I am going to go tonight and face the music. I will take the test and suffer the consequences of my bad choice not to study. Oh, Dorothy just said to go and study in the other room. Thank goodness for Dorothy, she really does make my education a priority. I pray that God will help me to be receptive to what I'm going to put in my mind."

The next day she wrote, "I am feeling much better today. I feel like the Lord rewarded me for being honest yesterday. I ended up with an 88 on my statistics test! And to think I was going to blow it off or lie to my teacher. Thank You, God, for helping me to make the right decisions."

Her relationship with her ex-husband has also been a struggle. He is incarcerated for abusing Vicki, but she has been co-dependent on him over seven years. She writes, "I let him beat me down so bad that I have very low self-esteem. That is another one of our issues to work on. I have let him control me so much and cause me to feel guilty and obligated to him. I thought it was my duty to take our children out to the penitentiary to visit their father. I have made progress in this area also. I have not been out there to see him for about a month. I have not accepted his calls or returned any of his letters. It's a very scary situation but I am going to put my trust in Christ and let him lead me."

Daisy's story is one that is not easy to tell because of all the incomprehensible emotional, physical, and spiritual pain she has endured. She grew up in a very dysfunctional family. Her mother died when she was 7 and her stepfather and step-sisters raised her. She was sent to foster homes, boarding schools, and ultimately ran away at age 15. She married at age 16, and had her first child at 17. The baby died at two weeks of age from causes related to Daisy's drinking problem. She had two more children and finally divorced her husband who abandoned them.

When Daisy was 21, she met another man, continued to drink a lot, and took drugs with him. He was very abusive to her, yet she had a son by him. There is now no communication between Daisy, her son, and his father.

When she was 25, Daisy had another girl but gave her up for adoption. Her third marriage to a man in prison was equally abusive. She has never divorced him because she fears physical retribution.

Tragically in 1995 Daisy was in a hit-and-run accident

that broke both her legs. Doctors were able to save both legs, and she is able to walk. Daisy came to Christian Women's Job Corps hoping to find a place to learn computer skills as well as learn God's Word. She has overcome her substance abuse problem and relies on her friends, family, church, and the Bible for support. She describes what she's learned: "I am a special person, and I have a future ahead. God loves me and will never leave me."

Daisy dreams that she will attend Interstate Business College and earn a computer information specialist degree. This will enable her to get off Social Security and be independent. She realizes, "I was spared for a reason. Maybe to be a missionary or help other people come out of the dark. I don't know, but I know I love Jesus. I have confidence and self-esteem and know I will make it this time with Jesus on my side." Daisy wants to break the vicious cycle of poverty that trapped her. By God's grace and power she is rising above all the terror and pain she has endured.

UNIQUELY BISMARCK

MARY'S STORY CAPTURES the struggles that many Native Americans face from living on reservations: limited job and education opportunities, health problems, poor family environment, and reliance on welfare to survive. North Dakota's Native American people are the descendants of the tribes of the Mandan, Hidasta, Arikara Nation, the Yanktonai, Wahpeton, and other Dakota (commonly known as Sioux) tribes. Through the years they have struggled for peace and overcome many challenges. Their history and culture are combined in a rich heritage that is often lost in their struggle for survival.

Welfare reform is a reality in the state capital, Bismarck. Single-parent families with children over the age of 3 must attend job training and apply for at least ten jobs weekly. County and state job placement workers as well as care providers working with those affected by welfare changes were asked by Southern Baptists, "What do you see to be your largest challenge?" They responded with three requests in this order:

1) professional and personal lifestyles skill training;

2) benevolent funding;
3) distributing items such as paper goods, soaps, personal items, used clothing for work, and used furniture. The need for the ministry of Christian Women's Job Corps was certainly evident.

In North Dakota, any woman on AFDC (Aid to Families with Dependent Children) has to find a part-time job, volunteer 20 hours a week, or apply for 40 jobs per week. Social Services, who administrates the AFDC program, ran out of community agencies to assign AFDC women to and asked the state government if it could include religious organizations. Not only did they change the law to include Christian agencies, but also declared church secretary positions eligible to fulfill the requirement of volunteer service. In addition, Social Services pays women for 20 hours of child care during their volunteer service.

The mission statement for Christian Women's Job Corps, housed in the BisMan Christian Community Center in Bismarck, is simple and straightforward:

• to reach low-income people for Christ and provide spiritual training and fellowship;
• to assist low-income and welfare participants to become independent and productive citizens by providing professional and personal living skill training using community resources and mission center personnel.

The community center shares offices with Green Thumb Employment and the State Entrepreneurship for Single Parents and Minorities office. There is also a training center for general office and data entry skills. It is open during the day for the jobs and entrepreneurship programs and in the evenings for other ministry opportunities.

The ministry is guided by the Christian Women's Job Corps Bismarck Task Force composed of Dorothy, a computer consultant, a job service consultant, a college instructor, and a high school teacher. They meet as needed and offer their expertise in these areas as they determine strategies for ministering to women in poverty.

The executive board for Christian Women's Job Corps is comprised of five local pastors, the associational director of missions, and five community leaders who are involved in business, community service, education, and insurance. They meet to direct the legal matters of Christian Women's Job Corps. Bismarck's Christian Women's Job Corps was granted 501(c)(3) status on September 3, 1997. This enables them to apply for grants through foundations and other charitable sources. It also validates the viability of such a program in Bismarck.

CWJC provides training programs through community agencies that fall within four categories: financial management, life skill development, job training, and education. Participants have access to financial management that teaches them about budgeting and maintaining a checking account. They have opportunity to gain life skills through a displaced homemaker and single parent program, parenting classes, or another life skills program that includes assertiveness, problem solving, self-esteem, nutrition, consumer skills, and stress management. Christian Women's Job Corps participants also have access to several forms of education such as GED; basic skills enhancement for math, reading, or composition; college preparation; computer literacy; drivers education; English as a second language; and literacy.

Financial assistance is available for Christian Women's Job Corps participants in several forms. The first is Job Corps—a training facility for youth. The second option is Job Training Program Assistance; a federally funded program that provides advanced classroom or college training. Third, On-the-Job Training reimburses employers part of a salary for a specified time while training employees. Fourth is Green Thumb Senior Employment, for seniors age 55 and older. It will pay participants' full salary to a community agency.

Christian Women's Job Corps also provides clothing and food, as the items are available. Rent assistance, furniture, and personal items have been supplied to several CWJC families. Their resources, however, are limited and they rely on gifts from individuals and churches in order to meet those needs.

Dorothy Longie describes how God provided for Christian Women's Job Corps as they set up an office skill-training center: "I started working on a budget for opening the training center. I would need $500 and a computer for upgrading keyboarding skills on a one-to-one basis. On Thursday, I brought our need to the Lord. No one knew about it. On Saturday, a couple from Orlando, Florida, called. The husband had been with a ministry team on the reservation where we were missionaries. He said, 'Dorothy, the Lord told me to send you $500.' I cried as I told him of my request to the Lord for $500 and we rejoiced together as we acknowledged the Lord's approval for our training centers." Christian Women's Job Corps now has three computers with tables and office chairs.

Stories abound giving testimony to the remarkable ways that God has provided for the center and ministry of Christian Women's Job Corps. In August 1997, Baptist Student Ministries students at Ridgecrest and Glorieta Conference Centers donated almost $4,000 to Christian Women's Job Corps in Bismarck. Trudy Johnson recommended to National Student Ministries that these offerings be designated to one Christian Women's Job Corps site, such as Bismarck. This money enabled Dorothy to hire Vicki to assist her in the work this year.

PEOPLE WHO MAKE A DIFFERENCE

Dorothy Longie has been involved in management for more than 30 years in automobile dealerships, motels, banks, and apartment complexes. Her experience is complemented by her involvement in missions ministries with her husband. She has served as a volunteer coordinator for the Rescue Mission in Billings, Montana, and also established a training and job placement center for recovering addicts. She established and operated a home for Native American teenaged mothers at Fort Totten, North Dakota. She also serves the Dakota Baptist State Fellowship as the volunteer coordinator. These experiences gave her the skills she needs now as the director of the BisMan Christian Community Center that offers the ministry of Christian Women's Job Corps.

Pam Scheerz is a computer programmer and teacher who volunteers with Christian Women's Job Corps. She serves as a computer consultant and has set up curriculum for CWJC. She has found that in giving of her time, she has also received much. "I am a full-time mother and also a member of Capitol

Heights Baptist Church here in Bismarck, North Dakota. This is my first experience working with Dorothy. I met Dorothy one Sunday at church. She had asked the fellowship to bring someone with computer experience so that she could get her training program that she had been praying for so many years off the ground.

"I decided to go up to her after the church service and visit with her about it. She shared with me more about what they were doing, and I told her I could help her with that. I didn't realize what I was saying at the time, I guess, but when I look back I am very thankful for what has been accomplished after I said yes. I was looking for some volunteer work that I could do for the Lord but I didn't have any idea where to start, until I met Dorothy. She has truly taught me what I needed to see and learn.

"I think of the Scripture verse where God talks about not loving in word, neither in tongue but in deed and in truth. I always thought my faith was more kind of like the talk than walk. I've never really had the guts to do something, never really had an idea what direction to go. I could never quite grasp that term *missionary work*, that term that is used so much in Baptist churches. I didn't really grab on to the word *mission* until I met Dorothy and she invited me to help her with her missions work. And her work was the work of establishing and initiating free training programs for women — women on welfare, women who are single parents. Some of those women are Christians, and some of them are not.

"I guess I felt so comfortable working with Dorothy because she was so confident in the Lord and confident in the vision that she had been given to develop this training center. Four months have passed since I said yes to Dorothy, and it took a lot of prayer and phone calls, lots of visiting on her part, and more prayer for her vision and the mission to begin. It was when we received three used computers that it really began. That's when my work really began as we set up the systems, loaded the software, assembled the computer disks, and got some things organized that needed to be organized."

Beth is another instructor who has degrees in both elementary and high school education. As a substitute teacher in the Bismarck school system, she has agreed to be available whenever possible to assist CWJC clients. She plans curriculum for any academic needs that a participant has for working with a tutor.

Donna teaches lifestyle classes at Christian Women's Job Corps. As one who has been homeless she is uniquely qualified to work with women in need. After her marriage fell apart, Donna found herself a single mother living at hospitality house with her two children. Living there helped her gain self-sufficiency and she launched a successful job search. Ultimately she found two part-time jobs, one that provided medical benefits. In November 1996, Donna became a homeowner. Donna is sustained by the fact that God has a plan for her life. Through these difficulties she has gained much wisdom and empathy for women who are trying to break away from their pasts and to find future hope.

The role of prayer

Dorothy and Raymond Longie have had their share of physical struggles. Raymond has diabetes, high blood pressure, and Parkinson's disease. In July 1996, Dorothy discovered that she had lung cancer and began chemotherapy and radiation. After extensive lung surgery, the doctors could not find any cancer. They are grateful for the personal miracles that God has provided in their lives through answered prayer. They also acknowledge that He has stirred people's hearts and channeled the resources to them, as they need them.

For the Bismarck CWJC, it would be appropriate to say that it was founded on prayer. Every aspect of the remarkable story of this Christian Women's Job Corps site is testimony to the power of prayer and the results of answered prayer.

Hope for the future

Dorothy and Ray Longie know that their health is a gift from the Lord. They also realize that they must find and equip others to carry on the work after them. They are currently awaiting renewal of a grant from the North American Mission Board that supplies rent for the community center as well as their housing. (Dorothy and Raymond are Mission Service Corps volunteers.)

Dorothy dreams of expanding the program with more computers by adding four or six more. She also hopes for additional teachers to help with Bible study or mentoring ministries. Dorothy also knows that it is important for additional churches to become involved in meeting the myriad of needs women in the community experience. She knows they have the abilities and the resources. She knows they are called to minister.

5

The
Remarkable Story of
Uptown Baptist Church
Christian Women's Job Corps

THE REMARKABLE STORY OF
UPTOWN BAPTIST CHURCH
CHRISTIAN WOMEN'S JOB CORPS

"But whoever is kind to the needy honors God" (Prov. 14:31). "She opens her arms to the poor and extends her hands to the needy" (Prov. 31:20).

WALKING INTO THE worship center of Uptown Baptist Church, one's senses are aroused by the sounds of joy and sights of diversity. Here is fellowship, true koinoinia; people from all imaginable language/ethnic-culture groups talking and embracing. Even a first-time visitor does not feel like a stranger here, for she is with family, the family of God. On one wall of the sanctuary hang banners of the name of Jesus in English, Spanish, Russian, Swahili, Ethiopian, Korean, and Vietnamese.

The Cobb family worships at Uptown Baptist Church. Lindsay and Mindy have lived in the inner city of Chicago for 20 years. Serving Christ as missionaries, the Cobbs have raised their three daughters near the multiethnic Uptown community. Committed, caring Mindy now serves as the Uptown CWJC℠ site coordinator. Church and community members are her missions field.

Karen and Aisha's sustaining friendship began when they met in an adult education program. They were two young women from the inner city struggling to rise above difficult life circumstances. Karen, a member of Uptown Baptist Church, invited Aisha to visit the church. Sharing Bible study and worship strengthened their friendship and their faith.

Karen and Aisha were invited to join the first Christian Women's Job Corps℠ job orientation class in January 1997. They were both employed, but dissatisfied with their work opportunities. Knowing their desire for something more, Mindy wanted Karen and Aisha to be part of the first class. Perhaps participation in CWJC could help the two friends realize their dreams.

The four-week Christian Women's Job Corps course gave these young women some valuable skills. Aisha says, "I learned how to budget my finances and write resumes. I learned how important resumes are to an employer. We did mock interviews that set up situations that would help us to know how to handle them. It gave me a totally new look at work. It's not just work anymore when you have God in the picture."

Karen says, "I always struggled with how to write resumes. Christian Women's Job Corps has helped me to be more confident and comfortable about job hunting and writing resumes."

Karen and Aisha have overcome difficult obstacles in their lives. Karen came from a family in which there was a lot of arguing before her parents separated. Her family did not support Karen's desire to go to church. They believed that she was being brainwashed, and tried to stop her from attending church.

Aisha knows what it is to face the anxiety of an unknown future. She miraculously was cured of cervical cancer before she received any treatment. These two women know that having several sources of support is vital for overcoming difficulties. As friends, they rely on one another. They call each other at work and keep one another apprised of job interviews. They both work as caregivers for Barbara's mother. Barbara is a member of the Uptown CWJC Task Force and a mentor. Barbara gives Karen and Aisha both practical and spiritual advice. The two young women also draw strength from fellowship, Bible study, and worship at Uptown Baptist Church.

These Scripture passages are significant to them, and as Karen says "they help me":

"But you are a chosen people, a royal priesthood, a holy nation, a people belonging to God, that you may declare the praises of him who called you out of the darkness into his wonderful light" (1 Peter 2:9).

"Search me O God, and know my heart; test me and know my anxious thoughts. See if there is any offensive way in me, and lead me in the everlasting way" (Psalm 139: 23–24).

Karen and Aisha realize that God has blessed them with gifts that are to be used for Him. Karen believes, "He has blessed me with patience and kindheartedness." Despite her difficult life circumstances and growing up in a cold, hard world, Karen's kind heart speaks to the remarkable power of God to transform a life.

Aisha describes God's blessings in her life, "He has blessed me with the ability to give my testimony. I find it easy to talk to people. Recently I shared with my mother."

One of the challenges that Karen and Aisha face is learning to set goals, small steps at a time, and then working to accomplish them. Karen's goals to be a chef and own a restaurant require her to go to college. She hopes to attend night classes at a college in the Chicago area. Aisha had a short-term goal to be a medical assistant and completed one last needed semester of training. She is now working full-time at a local hospital. Her long-term goal is to become a physician and use her hands to heal others.

HOW DID CWJC GET STARTED AT UPTOWN BAPTIST CHURCH?

UPTOWN'S CHRISTIAN WOMEN'S JOB CORPS formed a task force. They wrote this mission statement: "Christian Women's Job Corps, a ministry of WMU, at Uptown Baptist Church seeks to:
1. help women find jobs;
2. disciple women;
3. provide women with training and support to keep a job and be a good worker." This vision guided their design of an orientation and job readiness training curriculum.

Guidelines were identified for a client and mentor covenant. Agreed-on expectations for a client provide the map for her journey from dependency to self-sufficiency. In a typical covenant the client and mentor set goals such as being prompt, keeping promises, communicating clearly with one another, and praying for and supporting one another. These principles specify parameters and expectations for the mentor/client relationship.

With a church task force, mission statement, covenants, Bible study, and training curriculum in place, Uptown's Christian Women's Job Corps became operational. Information about the Christian Women's Job Corps shared in the church newsletter drew interest from women within the church. Six of them participated in the first training session.

How does it work?

MOST OF THE WOMEN invited to participate in CWJC are already involved in a Bible study at the church. However, clients and mentors also participate in Bible study together. At Uptown, the matching of a client with her mentor may either occur when a client begins the job orientation training or following the training during job placement.

Clients and mentors meet each Sunday afternoon for a month to study the curriculum. Task force members and mentors lead the training by using lecture, discussion, and role play. Training focuses on discovering marketable skills; preparing for interviews; preparing a resume and cover letter; filling out applications for housing or employment; budgeting; identifying resources for child care; arranging transportation; managing time; and conducting oneself in the workplace.

The remarkable difference CWJC makes

ON A TYPICAL SUNDAY evening in a church basement classroom, a CWJC job training session takes place. Diann, a task force member, conducts a lesson on completing job and housing applications. Line by line Diann carefully explains what each question is asking. The type and amount of information they must supply overwhelms most of the clients. They listen carefully, though, because they are determined to improve their life circumstances and break out of the cycle of dependency.

As the project coordinator for Christian Women's Job Corps, Mindy Cobb uses her gifts of teaching and encouragement to help change the lives of women in need. By virtue of her role as missionary, as well as her commitment to Uptown Baptist, she has a rich grasp of people, their needs, and what they can contribute to the ministry. Her dream for Christian Women's Job Corps is that "we could find jobs for every woman in Chicago who wanted to work."

Mindy tells a story that captures the essence of Christian Women's Job Corps: "Amy had never worked in her life. She came to our Christian Women's Job Corps training every week for four Sunday nights. She filled out an application for a factory and started working from 9:00 to 5:00 every day. After the first week, Amy decided she needed to take her grandma to the doctor. She called me after she took off to let me know. Of course, I told her to not miss any more days because she had just started a new job. Amy went back to work the next day, but then decided to visit her children the following day, so she took off again. When Amy returned to work, they told her they didn't need her anymore. Amy called me, and we went to lunch and talked about what happened and why it happened. She was shocked they fired her because she called in both times. To me, Christian Women's Job Corps is all about stopping the poverty cycle—showing women they are capable and worthy and that God really wants more for them. Amy's story may not sound successful, but it's a beginning and she has a taste of what it could be like."

Within Uptown Baptist Church and its community are women striving to pull their lives together. They are trusting God to help them. Through an informal network that has operated for almost 20 years, church members have referred several women to jobs in landscaping, child care, and the nursing field. How great is the need! How promising is the hope for self-sufficiency through Uptown's Christian Women's Job Corps!

UNIQUELY UPTOWN

ALONG THE NORTHERN Chicago Lake Michigan coast, just five

miles from the downtown loop, is the Uptown community. This inner-city, urban area is best described by the words *density* and *diversity*. It is estimated that 100,000 people line within a ten-square-block area. Of those who call Uptown home, 25,000 are senior adults, 14,000 are deinstitutionalized mental rehabilitation patients living in one of many halfway houses, and 15,000 of Chicago's estimated 40,000 homeless. Approximately half of Uptown's population is single-parent families.

It would be difficult to find a major ethnic group that is not represented in Uptown. The ethnic diversity of the community is evident in the local high school where students from 55 countries are enrolled. The students speak 35 primary languages.

Social and economic diversity characterizes Uptown as well. The affluence of Chicago's Lake Shore Drive is just blocks from the poverty and homelessness of this community. The number of families with public school children receiving public assistance is an estimated 80 percent.

Uptown Baptist Church was a natural choice for a CWJC pilot site. The church is a community-based congregation committed to rebuilding the inner city. The church's ministry philosophy of meeting individuals' physical, social, emotional, and spiritual needs while challenging them toward growth mirrors that of Christian Women's Job Corps.

The history of Uptown Baptist Church speaks to the initial commitment of Christians to build a church whose ministry would stand as a symbol of hope and light in a community struggling with darkness and hopelessness. Jim Queen, a boyhood resident of Uptown, came as a seminary graduate to plant a church in the community in 1976. Through the support of the Chicago Metropolitan Baptist Association, the Home Mission Board (now the North American Mission Board), Woman's Missionary Union®, and many churches, Uptown Baptist Church began to reach out to the community with Christ's compassion and love.

In 1979, Uptown Baptist Church (UBC) began to pursue a permanent home for the church. "Beginning in March 1979, UBC held monthly community praise services in a rented church building. We wanted to buy the building. In

November 1980, I made one last appeal to their church board asking them to consider selling their building." Jim Queen remembers, "They had no plans to sell." God had other plans; and by March 1981, UBC had a permanent home and was constituted on September 27, 1981. Uptown Baptist's resolute vision to reach out to the community is the framework on which Christian Women's Job Corps is built.

Women in Chicago face many challenges such as unemployment or working for low wages while the cost of living escalates. Many women who have children cannot find affordable child care. Welfare reform is now forcing women to deal with the realities of a system that often works against them. It is often difficult for women who have a low sense of self-worth to fill out employment applications. Often lacking the skills or education to perform the job, they continue to be disappointed when denied employment.

As in many cities, some Uptown women struggle with multiple problems such as mental illness, addictions, a poverty mind-set, and a spirit of hopelessness. Each problem requires attention, and the combination of several problems often presents a complex challenge.

PEOPLE WHO MAKE A DIFFERENCE

CWJC SITE COORDINATOR Mindy Cobb serves with a church task force of Mona Everest, Diann Lambrecht, Mary Thompkins, and Barb Ziermann. Each woman is a member of Uptown Baptist Church and brings her own experience to the task force. Each woman also serves as a mentor.

Mona felt a clear call to minister to the poor, and found a place of service at Uptown. She saw the need for mentoring, job placement, job training, and follow-up. Her gifts of encouragement, mercy, service, hospitality, and teaching enable her to be a task force leader. Mona believes that "developing personal relationships with women in need and long-term follow-through are keys to enable them to actually take steps forward in their lives." Her dream is that Christian Women's Job Corps will become a significant force in Uptown.

Fifteen years ago, Barb responded to God's call to move from business to social work in an urban setting. Her gifts of mercy and administration enable her to assist and encourage women in their first jobs, as well as plan curriculum for the Christian Women's Job Corps training. She hired Karen and Aisha to work as caregivers with her mother and is able to guide these young women regarding practical matters, housekeeping skills, practicing assertiveness, and spiritual concerns. Her dream is to involve women from other churches and begin a day-care service.

THE ROLE OF PRAYER

PRAYER IS A foundation upon which the ministry of Uptown Baptist Church and its Christian Women's Job Corps are built. Church members pray for each other and their hurting community. Mentor and clients pray together. Interested and concerned Christians outside Chicago make a difference in Uptown through their prayers.

HOPE FOR THE FUTURE

UPTOWN'S CHRISTIAN WOMEN'S JOB CORPS faces some obstacles. They need financial support to hire a staff member to facilitate the ministry. They need more trained mentors and additional instructors for their growing program. Ultimately, this means locating multiple resources, and having the time to network.

Mindy's ministry at Uptown Baptist extends beyond CWJC and she cannot invest as much time in the ministry as she would like. Since Christian Women's Job Corps at Uptown also attempts to locate possible jobs for participants, the task force hopes to find someone who will assist participants in job searches.

Mindy shares, "We are progressing slowly but surely. We have a small amount of volunteers to call on and they don't have much time left over. In the city most of the ladies in our church work long hours and have demanding jobs. We have very few retired healthy people who have the time, energy, and resources that many churches take for granted. We are excited about this ministry and believe God is going to change lives through the Christian Women's Job Corps. We look forward to what God is going to do next and are ready to be used by Him."

Christian Women's Job Corps at Uptown Baptist Church is one of many creative, relevant ministries of the church. The church's vision for reaching the community is critical to this ministry. Remarkable, here is hope in a hopeless place.

"With all your heart you must trust the Lord and not your own judgment. Always let him lead you, and he will clear the road for you to follow" (Prov. 3:5–6 CEV).

6

....

*The
Remarkable Future
of
Christian Women's Job Corps*

THE REMARKABLE FUTURE OF CHRISTIAN WOMEN'S JOB CORPS

"Don't worry and ask yourselves, 'Will we have anything to eat? Will we have anything to drink? Will we have any clothes to wear?' Only people who don't know God are always worrying about such things. Your Father in heaven knows that you need all of these. But more than anything else, put God's work first and do what he wants. Then the other things will be yours as well" (Matt. 6:31–33 CEV).

CHRISTIAN WOMEN'S JOB CORPS^{SM} is an ongoing, dynamic process. By principle, CWJC^{SM} is focused on individual women and meeting their needs. Whether designed like South Carolina's one-on-one plan, a classroom approach like San Antonio, or a church-based community ministry like Uptown in Chicago, each CWJC site requires tremendous coordination of people, time, money, and resources. This chapter looks into the future of Christian Women's Job Corps as two sites learn from the experiences of pilot sites.

The Remarkable Washington, D.C. Christian Women's Job Corps

ONE SUNDAY, Dusty Minnis heard a sermon that changed her life. Sammy Campbell, at that time the director of the Johenning Baptist Community Center (JBCC) in southeast

Washington, D.C., was preaching. He spoke about the challenges facing the center. How could they best meet the needs of women and children in the community?

Dusty knew that God had His hand on her. She had grown up in southeast Washington, watching a beautiful neighborhood decline. A police officer, Dusty was all too familiar with gang battles and violence. Consequently she understood what Sammy was talking about. God had been preparing Dusty's heart through prayer. The Holy Spirit confirmed it with Scriptures that she couldn't get out of her mind.

On that Sunday, Dusty became passionate about helping women. She sensed that God wanted her to go to Johenning Baptist Community Center. Speaking with Sammy Campbell, she shared her passion with him. Dusty says, "Be careful what you pray about because the Lord will bring it about." Today she is the project coordinator for Johenning's Christian Women's Job Corps!

"God said to me, 'What do you see?' And I responded, 'I see cardboard people. They are walking dead.' And God said, 'So, give these people back their lives, give them back southeast Washington.'"

Dusty began leading a Bible study on Saturday mornings with women preparing to take the General Educational Development test (GED) at Johenning Baptist Community Center. She also worked in a 12-week course for at-risk youth called Sisters. Then Dusty was invited to a meeting about Christian Women's Job Corps. At that meeting, she wondered why she was there until she was asked to write their manual on mentoring. Dusty also served on the state Christian Women's Job Corps task force that began defining what shape the ministry would take. Beyond a doubt, Dusty knows that God called her to full-time ministry at the JBCC.

How did CWJC get started at Johenning?

Sammy Campbell (now serving with Alabama's Birmingham Baptist Association) had a vision for the women of Washington Highlands. He wanted them to be able to break the poverty cycle that had ensnared so many of them. As director of the JOBS (Job Opportunity Bank Services) program at Johenning Baptist Community Center, he wanted Johenning to be part of Christian Women's Job Corps as soon as he heard about it. JOBS offered an existing network and served as a template for designing this Christian Women's Job Corps site.

The JOBS program has three elements: academic assessment, entrepreneurial opportunities, and participants' job acceptance through the efforts of JOBS. They must volunteer up to four hours a week for two years. This program encourages participants to continue to meet with support groups, as well as provide an opportunity for them to reciprocate some of what they received through JOBS.

How does it work?

The mission statement for Christian Women's Job Corps at Johenning Baptist Community Center is: To empower women who are in a cycle of poverty to gain skills for life, to increase their ability to obtain and sustain employment, and to develop a vision for success, all within a Christian context.

When a woman applies to the JBCC Christian Women's Job Corps she undergoes a group orientation. Several evaluations occur at this time: an education evaluation, a pre-employment assessment, and a support group assignment. Women then have an opportunity to choose whether they enter a pre-GED or a GED program.

During the job training phase, participants enter a support group. They also begin classroom training with job skills development and job search. If they are hired for a job, they are given on-site training. Once they have a job, women have a chance to continue in their support groups, as well as volunteer their time at Johenning. These two strengthen a woman's potential to sustain success on the jobs.

The remarkable difference CWJC makes

Vernetta has lived across the street from Johenning for nearly 17 years. Still, she did not realize that the community center had something to offer her. That changed when someone from the community center came by to visit her, accompanied by a realtor who offered Vernetta the chance to buy her rental home. She was also offered an opportunity to own her own business and take her GED. Vernetta shares, "Because of you, I now have what you all have. Because of your efforts, I have secured my salvation and have established a relationship with Jesus Christ. May God continue to bless the Christian Women's Job Corps's efforts to reach and reclaim precious human lives for Christ."

UNIQUELY JOHENNING

ALMOST 45 YEARS ago Anna B. Johenning began a ministry to neighborhood children in her living room. The Johenning Baptist Community Center has grown from those humble beginnings to become a vital community service provider. The center places an important emphasis on building an effective community system that empowers families in Washington Highlands to soar above human difficulties. Four things drive the ministry of Johenning today: spiritual development, community planning, community involvement, and individual responsibility. The center's programs create support systems for adults, children, youth, and families through outreach and counseling.

Roughly 40,000 people, half of them children, call Washington Highlands home. The primarily African-American community has a high density of substandard housing, predominately multifamily dwellings. Only 55 percent of adults over 25 have finished high school. Unemployment is high and those who do work receive only minimum wage. More than 35 percent of Washington Highlands' residents live below the poverty line. Single parents head most households and 60 percent of those are women with dependent children.

It is a community riddled with violence. More than 70 percent of the crimes committed are assaults. In the midst of this sea of hurting humanity, Johenning is a safe harbor, a source of hope. Johenning offers Washington Highlands Christ's empowering love. Christian Women's Job Corps is one of the sources of hope offered to young women who desire a life of self-sufficiency.

Johenning Baptist Community Center and Christian Women's Job Corps believe that support groups are a vital part of the ministry. The poverty in Washington Highlands is pervasive and impacts people's hopes, desires, dreams, and visions. There is also a great lack of trust. Many of these people have been victims of neglect from the government as well as other community agencies. Trust must be built.

Participating in a support group allows women to become dependent on one another. It allows them to become familiar with people outside the community who want to help. Life skills are also taught to those in support groups. Some of the topics addressed include: parenting skills; nutrition; banking and financial management; conflict resolution; developing and maintaining healthy relationships; purchasing a home; dressing for success and interviewing; saving for college education; as well as table etiquette.

Participants also have an opportunity to study the Bible. The CWJC manual says that Christian Women's Job Corps hopes that participants will "come to understand that transformation of life comes only through accepting Jesus Christ as Lord and Savior of their lives. The participants will learn who they are and the power that dwells within them as they receive Jesus and allow the Spirit to work out the will of God for their lives."

Through support groups, participants will have an opportunity to go on field trips. They may go to museums; on shopping trips; to plays, art galleries, or special concerts. Leaders hope this will give participants a chance to see new options for their own lives.

Christian Women's Job Corps of Johenning Baptist Community Center has very clearly stated expectations for its participants. They are modeling tough love for these women, preparing them for employment. Women are expected to be on time, to refrain from inappropriate behavior, and to keep alcohol or illegal drugs away from the center. When participants sign their covenants, they are agreeing to these positive behaviors. Dusty believes that it is important for women to learn that some actions are not acceptable in the workplace, and they are not acceptable in Christian Women's Job Corps.

PEOPLE WHO MAKE A DIFFERENCE

AS THE PROJECT coordinator for CWJC, Dusty is still gathering all the resources together. She is identifying people for instructor positions and people with specific skills that will enhance the mentoring process. The task of project coordinator requires her to know the mission of the organization, how it will be accomplished, what resources are available, how to access additional resources, and how to prepare and train workers for volunteering and mentoring. She has learned it takes time to pull everything together.

At this writing, the Christian Women's Job Corps project is nearly ready to be launched. Dusty's description of people with the potential to be involved with meeting the needs of women speaks to the way that God brings the right people together in His time. Dusty is identifying skills and gifts of people and sharing the vision of CWJC with them. Here are some of those people who are praying about working with Christian Women's Job Corps.

Dusty intends to approach someone who owns some apartments about using them as transitional housing for Christian Women's Job Corps participants. She also knows a couple who helped set up a catering business at Johenning Center. Entrepreneurship is one of the options for women who are trying to break out of poverty. Dusty also has identified a librarian, a social worker, and a cosmetologist who are all praying about how God wants to use them.

Sarah Higgenbotham who serves on the task force has an interest in teaching women how to use computers. A computer lab is being set up with networked computers and Internet access. Christian Women's Job Corps at JBCC values computer literacy as one of the skills that women will gain. God continues to move people toward the ministry of Christian Women's Job Corps.

THE ROLE OF PRAYER

DUSTY'S APPROACH OF recruiting others to minister through Johenning's CWJC is testimony to her belief in the power of prayer! The remarkable stories that will come out of Washington Heights will no doubt reflect His people putting His work first as they do what He wants.

HOPE FOR THE FUTURE

DUSTY IS A WOMAN compelled by God to serve Washington

Highlands. Her dream is that in five years the women who have come through Christian Women's Job Corps will be in charge of their own lives. "These women are strong enough to do it; they have survived hell. I'm a retired D.C. police officer. I know how they have had to survive. I know that at 3:00 A.M. on a muggy summer morning when it's 85°F in the shade, that its about 150°F in those cracker box houses. Everybody is outside trying to get cool. Otherwise somebody is going to get on somebody's nerves. These women know how to survive. They can do it."

Together with the other ministries of JBCC, Christian Women's Job Corps hopes to impact the Washington Highlands neighborhood with God's empowering and redeeming love. He is calling people forth, equipping them, and giving them the resources to remarkably accomplish His task.

The Remarkable Story of Nashville's Christian Women's Job Corps

"When you beg the Lord for help, he will answer, 'Here I am!' Don't mistreat others or falsely accuse them or say something cruel. Give your food to the hungry and care for the homeless. Then your light will shine in the dark; your darkest hour will be like the noonday sun" (Isa. 58: 9–10 CEV).

CHRISTIAN WOMEN'S JOB CORPS is "taking your everyday, ordinary life...and place it before God as an offering" (Rom. 12:1–2 *The Message*). This is the story of ordinary women and men in Nashville whom God has called. They are willing to give their lives as offerings as they reach out to women in poverty.

HOW DID CWJC GET STARTED IN NASHVILLE?
CHRISTIAN WOMEN'S JOB CORPS of Nashville was launched in September 1997. It began with God moving in the hearts of several men and women. In the summer of 1994, Creely Wilson, associational WMU director for Nashville Metro Association, attended a conference at Ridgecrest Baptist Conference Center during Woman's Missionary Union Week.

It was there that she learned about the pilot projects of Christian Women's Job Corps. Creely's interest in the new ministry of WMU was piqued. Eighteen months later, she learned about the first National Certification Training in Birmingham; and with assistance from the associational WMU, she took Diane Shepherd and Janice Cox, both from Nashville, to the training with her.

On September 11, the first Nashville Christian Women's Job Corps Task Force met to hear about the ministry: the project, its history, the pilot sites, and the strategy for CWJC in Nashville. Diane shared that God was building a house in Nashville and the task force's role was to help design the structure. This metaphor helped shape the thinking of the task force as they planned.

A tentative organizational chart was presented at that meeting, and task force members were asked to pray about their role in building the house of Christian Women's Job Corps. They were given options for involvement: serving on the task force, praying for the ministry, offering gifts and abilities, enlisting others to serve, and being an advocate for Christian Women's Job Corps by asking others to support the ministry.

At this writing, new names are being added weekly to the organizational chart filling needed responsibilities. There are nine coordinator positions for prayer, mentors, volunteers, celebrations, finances, evaluation, resource development, public relations, and education. Within each of those positions there are also specific assignments.

For 30 days following the initial task force meeting, Diane and Creely spent many hours building the foundation of the house. First, a location for Christian Women's Job Corps was selected and approved at a church in east Nashville—Lockeland Baptist Church. Their pastor, John Langlois, serves as a consultant to the task force. A former Sunday School department was converted into the headquarters for Christian Women's Job Corps. The room was repainted, floors refinished, and furniture from a going-out-of-business sale has been moved upstairs.

Another event during these 30 days was the first mentor training for the association. About 35 men and women came to Lockeland Baptist Church for a three-hour orientation and training session. Sheri Carroll from Families First, Tennessee's welfare to work plan, was one of the presenters, creating a profile of these women and what their challenges are. The second hour of mentor training focused specifically on defining the role of the mentor, the nature of cross-cultural ministry, and how to communicate effectively. Those who came for the training were interested volunteers and mentors, associational WMU leadership, Mission Service Corps volunteers, and church staff members.

In just 30 days Christian Women's Job Corps moved into its site, conducted mentor training, developed its overall plan for ministry, and enlisted people to fill coordinators positions. Nashville still faces many challenges such as coordinating schedules to find time to meet, communicating the essence of Christian Women's Job Corps to churches, finding funds to support the ongoing ministry, and enlisting volunteers and mentors to work with participants. Diane still works part-time at Lockeland Baptist Church, but her heart's desire is to focus on Christian Women's Job Corps full-time.

HOW DOES IT WORK?

THE NASHVILLE CHRISTIAN WOMEN'S JOB CORPS working mission statement summarizes the kind of house that they are building for the Lord: Believing that many women in poverty feel hopeless about breaking out of the welfare cycle due to real barriers that prevent them from employment networks, and that Jesus Christ calls us to care for "the least of these" with unconditional love, we will exercise stewardship of God's gifts that compel us to enable others to unleash their God-given potential.

Christian Women's Job Corps seeks to empower women who are in a cycle of poverty:
• to gain professional and personal skills for life;
• to enhance their ability to obtain and sustain employment for self sufficiency;
• to develop vision for life by linking them in a Christian context with people who value them.

Tennessee officials have responded to the changes brought about by welfare reform through Families First.

Families on welfare must now spend 20 hours a week looking for a job and 20 hours a week in job training. Christian Women's Job Corps in Nashville is seeking approval from Families First as a job training facility. If they receive this approval, participants may count their time spent at Christian Women's Job Corps as a part of their job training. The task force realizes this is a critical step for the ministry, and it awaits approval from Families First. In order to seek approval, Diane and Creely spent many hours creating a document that summarizes what this "house" will look like.

Christian Women's Job Corps in Nashville intends to focus on each woman's needs with a goal of empowerment. There are seven components to the ministry. First, the mentoring relationship is the nucleus of the program. The mentor/participant relationship allows the staff to accurately assess needs, evaluate progress, and nurture the participant as she reconnects with society and begins to move toward specific goals.

Second, One-on-One is a curriculum component that offers customized learning according to a woman's specific needs in the areas of self-confidence, personal awareness, and problem solving. Third, Helping Hands assists Christian Women's Job Corps participants with professional clothing, emergency food, transportation, and temporary child care. Fourth, a participant goes through intake where assessments are conducted and an individual development plan is created. The participant creates this plan with guidance from the intake team.

Activities are the fifth component. Participants are involved in both group and individual activities such as special workshops, field trips, and celebrations. Next, evaluations among participants, the program, and the community occur. This enables Christian Women's Job Corps staff to discern any adjustments that are necessary to make in the ministry. Finally, participants will attend classes three days a week at the classroom for Christian Women's Job Corps at Lockeland Baptist Church.

The planned curriculum addresses five areas: communication, computer lab, principles for living, career planning, and One-On-One — a curriculum component that offers customized learning according to a specific woman's needs. These five areas are covered in other job training programs and are commensurate with their curriculum. Participants will spend three hours a week in each subject area. Curriculum for principles for living is currently being explored.

During mentor training, women were challenged to consider taking that step of faith needed to enter into a helping relationship with a woman in need. Each mentor is required to enlist at least five prayer partners to support her in this ministry. Christian Women's Job Corps pilot projects demonstrated that prayer is a cornerstone to the mentoring relationship. Mentors and participants meet once a week for Bible study and prayer. Together they will establish a covenant that spells out specific goals and expectations of their relationship. Mentors are encouraged to maintain a journal of what they are learning and feeling. Mentors will meet monthly as a support group for one another. During this time, there will be prayer and Bible study as well as skill development. Mentors also report monthly to the project coordinator, giving an update of each participant's progress.

The mentoring relationship so vital to Christian Women's Job Corps is unique to many other job training programs. Walking beside a woman who is trying to break the cycle of poverty is a powerful tool for spiritual transformation. This is the same concept that Jesus demonstrated for us. He is Immanuel—"God with us." Mentoring someone means valuing her, empowering her, praying for her, encouraging her, advocating for her, teaching her, accepting her, and much more. At the heart of mentoring is the idea that Jesus mentored His disciples. He sent us His Spirit as the Power we can rely on as we mentor others.

UNIQUELY NASHVILLE

THIS OVERVIEW FROM the Nashville Christian Women's Job Corps manual summarizes the potential that CWJC in Nashville eagerly awaits: "It is a part of the Nashville Baptist Association which consists of 162 local churches, an excellent resource for creating an effective volunteer network. Although volunteer recruitment is neither denominationally

nor gender exclusive, many professional women from our
Baptist churches are willing to offer their time and expertise
to Christian Women's Job Corps as mentors and instructors.
Their involvement will certainly accentuate the high standard of excellence we have set for ourselves. As women
choose to be participants of Christian Women's Job Corps,
they will discover the emotional and spiritual support needed to sustain success, which is precisely what welfare reform
is attempting to accomplish."

PEOPLE WHO MAKE A DIFFERENCE

DIANE SHEPHERD IS involved in the inner-city ministry of
Woodcock Baptist Church. Janice Cox has also been involved
in the Woodcock ministry. Prior to attending the CWJC
National Certification Training event, their minds and hearts
were dreaming about what might be possible for a Christian
Women's Job Corps in Nashville. At the training in
Birmingham they heard from many that had piloted
Christian Women's Job Corps. The training gave them the
resources needed to begin the groundwork for establishing a
similar ministry. Creely is the Christian Women's Job Corps
Tennessee state coordinator, and in this role she will serve as
a resource to Christian Women's Job Corps in the state.

Prior to ever hearing about Christian Women's Job Corps,
God had challenged Diane to be involved in helping women
break the cycle of poverty. Her own personal ministry in east
Nashville reflected this as she mentored women in poverty.
Her contacts and her commitment were crucial to building
the foundation for Nashville's Christian Women's Job Corps.
Diane is the project coordinator for this new site.

HOPE FOR THE FUTURE

IN NASHVILLE THERE is great intensity at each task force meeting as reports are made, resources are identified, provisions
are described, and God's answered prayers become evident.
At this writing, Nashville Christian Women's Job Corps in is
on the verge of assigning mentors and clients. The task force
faithfully believes that God will grant them the wisdom needed as they take this first important step.

Developers of this new CWJC site have drawn great

strength and support from all of the pilot sites as existing mentor and project manuals have been scanned, and resources are gleaned. The emotional and spiritual support from other pilot sites and the national WMU also illustrate the potential power of the developing Christian Women's Job Corps network. Women all across the United States involved in this remarkable ministry will be connected through participating in this life-changing ministry. Women in need will be no longer forgotten as long as Christian Women's Job Corps draws Christians to be actively involved with women who are breaking free of dependency and moving toward self-sufficient lives filled with hope.

7

....

The
Biblical and Theological
Foundation
for
Christian Women's Job Corps

THE BIBLICAL AND THEOLOGICAL FOUNDATION
FOR
CHRISTIAN WOMEN'S JOB CORPS
by C. Anne Davis

CHRISTIAN WOMEN'S JOB CORPS[SM], a ministry of Woman's Missionary Union®, provides a Christian context in which women in need are equipped for life and employment. This ministry takes place in a missions context through which women help women. The aim of this chapter is to suggest biblical and theological foundations on which involvement in such a ministry as Christian Women's Job Corps (CWJC[SM]) rest. In other words, why should women become involved in helping women in poverty become self-sustaining through the CWJC?

The "why" question should surface early in any ministry endeavor undertaken by Christians. It should surface early because the way we address the "why" question will then become the touchstone which keeps our motivation alive and guides our every action.

Personnel involved in developing each CWJC site will work out their own biblical and theological reasons, and these need to be clearly articulated. This necessitates working on definitions such as:
1. What is a "Christian context?"
2. What is a "missions context?"

This process of working out a biblical and theological rationale for involvement in Christian Women's Job Corps also requires a foundation in Scripture. I will suggest several Old Testament themes and New Testament teachings and events that I hope will provide a starting place for working out biblical foundations for ministry.

These suggestions are the results of many conversations with colleagues, my study of Scripture, and my own experiences in ministry. However, I must especially acknowledge my indebtedness to Patricia L. Bailey, executive director of the Advocacy Center for Victims of Crime, Waco, Texas, who has challenged me to think about these issues and understand more of Who God is and what God expects of me.

OLD TESTAMENT

TWO PERVASIVE THEMES in the Old Testament have major implications for our involvement in Christian Women's Job Corps. Each of these outlines ways God's people are to respond to those in society who are poor or otherwise vulnerable. One of these themes focuses on meeting the needs of individuals for the daily essentials of life such as food, clothing, and shelter. The other theme relates to social justice or fair treatment for all people in their interactions with the structures and institutions of society.

John Havlik, a former director of evangelism at the North American Mission Board (formerly the Home Mission Board) said it best. "It is strange that many evangelicals who defend the inspiration of the Old Testament are blind to its teachings about social justice/righteousness and the will of God concerning social justice. In the Kingdom of God that was, is, and is to come, there are social goals that involve all of human life in society. God's concern and compassion have always included social goals and those goals are clearly indicated to be the goals of the community of faith."[1]

WELFARE OF INDIVIDUALS

EXODUS 20–23, Leviticus 17–26, and Deuteronomy 12–26 are examples of the many Old Testament Scriptures that describe the provisions believers in Yahweh are to make for the poor and the disadvantaged. Positive acts of caring should be offered to all "those falling on hard times" which includes brothers and sisters, neighbors, sojourners or foreigners, people of another nationality who are temporarily living in the community, as well as widows and orphans. These categories comprise the classical listing of persons in need at that time in history.

Robert Morris describes the concept of "caring for the stranger" as one of the most revolutionary concepts of Hebrew Scriptures. He states that about 800 B.C., "it was possible to reduce an oral tradition to written form in which one persistent theme was the injunction to help the helpless."[2] What is revolutionary, in Morris's opinion, is that the Hebrews introduced a proactive caring into a world that defined caring as "not doing someone harm."

Israel's welfare laws were founded on this kind of caring for the vulnerable and strangers in the community. They were designed to provide essentials for daily life to those who were destitute and disenfranchised, and in so doing to offer them an opportunity to become self-sufficient. These provisions of welfare testify to the nature and character of God and the seriousness with which Israel approached the responsibility of helping others. Examples of these welfare provisions included, but were not limited to, the following:

1. Seventh-Year Release

Every seventh year, the poor fellow countrymen were released from their debts. It was God's intention that everyone would get a chance to start over and would not be doomed to debt forever. "At the end of every seventh year you must make a remission of debts. This is how it is to be made; everyone who holds a pledge shall return the pledge of the person indebted to him. He must not press a fellow-countryman for repayment, for the Lord's year of remission has been declared" (Deut. 15:1–2).

In addition, the admonition to help the poor is further spelled out in verses 7 and 8 of Deuteronomy 15. These verses read as follows: "If there is a poor man with you, in any of your towns in your land which the Lord your God is giving to you, you shall not harden your heart, nor close your hand from your poor brother; but you shall freely open your hand to him, and shall generously lend him sufficient for his need in whatever he lacks" (NASB). These verses not only spelled out God's expectation that the believers should help, but they also made clear that believers were to help with compassion and generosity. It is clear here that God did not intend for any needs to be left unmet.

2. Loaning of Money

Provision was made for interest-free loans to be made to people who were poor. Exodus 22:25 reads: "If you lend money to my people, to the poor among you, you are not to act as a creditor to him; you shall not charge him interest" (NASB). Even if people borrowed money and used their coats as collateral, the lender was obligated to give the coats back before sundown since it was the poor people's only means of staying warm. This matter is addressed in verses 26–27 of Exodus 22. The issue here seems to be that God did not intend His children to make a profit from the help they offered to the poor.

3. Profit on the Sale of Food

In verses 35–40 of Leviticus 25, items one and two of this list are reviewed and there is the additional statement that people were not to profit from the sale of food to their fellow countrymen who were poor.

4. Harvesting Rules for the Poor

"When you reap the harvest of your land, you shall not reap your field to its very border, neither shall you gather the gleanings after your harvest. And you shall not strip your vineyard bare, neither shall you gather the fallen grapes of your vineyard; you shall leave them for the poor and for the sojourner; I am the Lord your God" (Lev. 19:9–11 RSV).

One of the major means of feeding the poor was to leave grain and fruit in the fields for them to gather. A well-known example of this can be found in the Book of Ruth. She and Naomi were living on welfare of their day. Since Ruth was an alien and poor, this was her only means of supporting herself when they first returned to Judah.

5. Seventh Year—The Fallow Year

In addition to instructing the farmers to leave grain in the fields for the poor, Exodus 23:10–11 adds the admonition that every seventh year, the farmers were to let their fields, vineyards, and groves lie fallow. The poor could then gather what grew in this seventh year.

6. Terms of Payment for Work

Deuteronomy 24:14–15 reads, "If you hire poor people to work for you, don't hold back their pay, whether they are Israelites or foreigners who live in your town. Pay them their wages at the end of each day, because they live in poverty and need the money to survive. If you don't pay them on time, they will complain about you to the Lord, and he will punish you" (CEV).

In this verse there is a clear note of empathy for the poor. When you hire someone, you are to pay them that day because it is all they will have to purchase food. God instructs the helpers to be kind and gentle with people who have fallen on hard times.

7. The Year of Jubilee

The year of Jubilee is noted in Leviticus 25:25–28. These verses record that if poor people have to sell their land in order to live through hard times, there are ways for the person to get back their land. Relatives could redeem the land; the poor person could later get enough money and buy it back; or during the year of Jubilee the land would automatically revert to the ownership of the poor people who were forced to sell it. Dwelling houses in walled cities were exempt from this Jubilee practice.

8. Harvest Rights of Sojourners, Widows, and Orphans

These populations were given special consideration related to harvesting crops. In Deuteronomy 24:17–22, the nation of Israel is warned to remember what it was like when they were slaves and poor in the land of Egypt. If a sheaf was forgotten in the field, it was to be left for the poor. The fruit of the olive tree was to be gathered by shaking the tree once not twice. What was left was for the poor and vulnerable people. Grapes missed on the first harvest were to be left for the poor.

9. Cities of Refuge

In Numbers 35:9–15, the Lord told Moses to set aside six cities for refuge where a person who unintentionally kills someone can flee for safety from avengers until the accused can stand before the congregation for judgment. These cities of refuge were for the children of Israel and the sojourners.

10. The Tithe of the Produce

Every third year a tithe of the produce was to be given to the priests, the sojourner, the fatherless, and the widow so they would have something to eat within the cities. In Deuteronomy 26:12–15, it is recorded that this tithe of the produce was a commandment of the Lord.

It becomes clear from these examples that the God of Israel was a God of compassion and mercy toward the poor and those who had fallen on hard times. God commanded the children of Israel to take care of those less fortunate in the community as well as those who would be passing through the community. These welfare laws were based on the notion that no needs were to go unmet as long as the community of believers had the resources provided to them by God.

SOCIAL JUSTICE ISSUES

THE CHRISTIAN LIFE of helping ought to be balanced between priestly and prophetic functions. The balance does not have to be present in each individual, but it does have to be present in the corporate body of the church.

Priestly helping is usually defined as that helping which takes place in a face-to-face encounter with another person, family, or small group. This kind of helping generally involves a relationship and shapes itself as the provision of resources, support, comfort, and encouragement. It is more like the individual helping ideas outlined in the previous section.

Prophetic helping, on the other hand, involves trying to bring about changes in societal structures which are oppressive to people. Social justice ministries are prophetic helping. These are harder to do and are often fraught with risks and dangers for the person(s) trying to bring about change. One example of a social justice issue is trying to rid our society of institutional racism.

Involving churches in priestly ministries is easier than involving them in prophetic ones. However, the church needs to be involved in bringing about social justice. For example, in Christian Women's Job Corps, priestly and prophetic ministries need to be addressed. Not only do we need to help women become employed and self-sufficient, we need to work to change the economic and political systems which are some of the roots of the continued poverty of single-mother families.

Part of the rationale for being involved in both kinds of helping is grounded in the reality of God. God is concerned about individual needs and with the structures and organizations of society which oppress people, especially the poor. The writings of the prophets clearly demonstrate God's displeasure with the nation of Israel when its justice system and its economic policies were oppressive toward the poor and those who had fallen on hard times. God sent the prophets to warn Israel that such injustices would not be tolerated, and those who perpetrated the injustice upon the people would have to stand before God's judgment.

The Book of Amos demonstrates this call to justice from God. Amos told the nation of Israel that they had trampled down the weak and helpless and pushed the poor out of the way (Amos 2:7). He further declared that at every place of worship, people slept on clothing that they had taken from the poor as security for debt (Amos 2:8). In chapter 3:5–7, Amos declared that Israel was doomed because it had twisted justice and cheated the weak and the poor people out of their rights. Israel had oppressed the poor and robbed them of their grain, taken bribes, and prevented the poor from getting justice in the courts (Amos 5:11–12).

In summary, Amos told Israel that they had failed the test of the plumb line; in light of their behavior toward the vulnerable people among them, God would not accept their worship or listen to their music. The only way that this situation was going to change, according to Amos, was if the people of Israel would "let justice roll down like waters and righteousness like an ever-flowing stream" (NASB).

NEW TESTAMENT

IN THE NEW TESTAMENT, the biblical mandates which direct Christians to be involved in such ministries as Christian Women's Job Corps are grounded in the life of Christ and His model of ministry, the kingdom of God, and the nature of the church.

LIFE AND MODEL OF THE MINISTRY OF CHRIST

THE EXAMPLE SET forth in the life of Christ is one that gives special attention to the poor. Jesus' actions serve to interpret His words, and His words interpret His actions. Author Donald Kraybill says, "Any gospel that is not social is not gospel. Jesus lived, interacted, and behaved in a real, social environment, disclosing God's social way."[3]

Nine descriptors outlined in the Book of Luke characterize Jesus' model of ministry. Jesus valued people more than religious traditions. Jesus included all people, especially the outcasts of society. Jesus required certain perspectives of His followers. The ministry of Jesus was saturated with love. Jesus set standards about how we are to treat each other. He specified proper attitudes for His followers to hold regarding wealth and possessions. He made clear the cost of discipleship. Jesus called His followers to persistent prayer. And He called all to repentance and salvation.

•Jesus brought good news to the poor.

Among the countless descriptions of Jesus preaching and ministering to the poor, four will be highlighted here. In Luke 4:18 Scripture records, "The spirit of the Lord is upon me, because the Lord has anointed me to preach the gospel to the poor" (RSV). Again in Luke 14:13–14, Jesus says, "But when you give a reception, invite the poor, the crippled, the lame, the blind, and you will be blessed, since they do not have the means to repay you; for you will be repaid at the resurrection of the righteous" (NASB).

In Matthew 11:5, the disciples are told to "Go and report to John what you hear and see: the blind receive sight and the lame walk, the lepers are cleansed and the deaf hear, and the dead are raised up, and the poor have the gospel preached to them" (NASB). Several chapters later in Matthew, a conversation is recorded between a young man and Jesus. The young man wanted to know what good deeds he must do to inherit eternal life. Jesus answered him. "If you wish to be complete, go and sell your possessions and give to the poor and you shall have treasures in heaven; and come, follow me" (Matt. 19:20–21 RSV).

• Jesus had serious conversations with the outcasts and powerless people.
Jesus talked with women, tax collectors, children, and other people who had been pushed out into the margin of society. In John 4, He talked with the woman at the well. His conversations with the tax collectors were numerous. In Mark 9: 36–37, Jesus told His disciples that whoever accepts a child in His name, accepts Him; He adds that whoever accepts Him accepts God.

• Jesus showed concern for the hungry people.
Time and time again in the New Testament, Jesus showed compassion for people who were hungry. In Mark 8, Jesus told His disciples that the crowd who had been with Him for three days had had nothing to eat. He knew that if He sent them away hungry, they would not have the strength to walk back to their homes.

• Jesus' life models for us compassion for the sick and mercy for those in need. He demonstrated a new way of life and a new way of treating people, especially the poor, vulnerable, and the oppressed.
However, Jesus did not stop with care for the hurts and struggles of the individual. He also called into question the structures and institutions of His society which declared some people unclean, which ignored human need, and which placed religious traditions ahead of the needs of people.

God's Love Was Not Only for Israel and Rich People
After Peter's experience at the home of Cornelius in Acts 10, he declared that "I most certainly understand now that God is not one to show partiality, but in every nation the man

who fears him and does what is right, is acceptable to him"(RSV). In James 2 it is recorded, "Show no partiality as you hold the faith of our Lord Jesus Christ, the Lord of glory. For as one with gold rings and in fine clothing comes into your assembly, and a poor one in shabby clothing also comes in, and you pay attention to the one who wears the fine clothing and say, 'Have a seat here, please,' while you say to the poor one, 'Stand there,' or 'Sit at my feet,' have you not made distinctions among yourselves, and become judges with evil thoughts? Listen, my beloved ones. Has not God chosen those who are poor in the world to be rich in the faith and heirs of the kingdom which God has promised to those who love God? But you have dishonored the poor one. Is it not the rich who oppress you?"(RSV).

JESUS SPOKE AGAINST RELIGIOUS RITUALS
THEN JESUS SPOKE to the multitudes and to His disciples saying, "The scribes and the Pharisees have seated themselves in the chair of Moses; . . . And they tie up heavy loads, and lay them on men's shoulders; but they themselves are unwilling to move them with so much as a finger" (Matt. 23: 1–4 NASB). Jesus healed on the Sabbath and did not require that His disciples fast and pray while He was with them.

PEOPLE ARE MORE IMPORTANT THAN THINGS
JESUS' RESPONSE TO the Pharisees when His disciples were caught breaking the law against gathering food on the Sabbath made His values clear. "Don't you know what the Scriptures mean when they say, "Instead of offering sacrifices to me, I want you to be merciful to others"? If you knew what this means, you would not condemn these innocent disciples of mine" (Matt. 12:7 CEV).

THE KINGDOM OF GOD
THE IDEA OF the kingdom of God is deeply rooted in the Old Testament, even though the actual phrase does not appear in the Old Testament Scriptures. It is central to the teaching of Jesus and is described as the reign of God in human life. Once a person accepts God's gift of grace to share in the kingdom, it becomes incumbent upon that individual to accept God's

invitation to extend the kingdom. Maston describes this as follows: "We promote His Kingdom as we extend His RIGHTEOUS reign not only in our own lives but also in the lives of others and the society in which we live. The Kingdom is God's supreme gift and man's supreme task."[4]

Guthrie puts it another way. "The Christian gospel is a social gospel. Christians are people who by definition are committed to social justice and a new social order. To be a Christian includes not only praying but working that God's will may be done and God's kingdom come on earth."[5] From beginning to end, the Bible proclaims a social-political gospel. It teaches that to believe in God, in Jesus, or in the Holy Spirit is to "rise up" and serve God by doing justice and working for a world that reflects the justice of the kingdom of God.

THE CHURCH

WHILE THE DEFINITION of the church as a body of baptized believers may be accurate in a descriptive sense, it does not do justice to the real nature of the church. According to Leonard, the church is "an incarnated community of those who receive the Word of God in Christ Jesus and seek to incarnate that Word in their own lives through the power of the Holy Spirit." He goes on to say, "The gospel provided the church with a new relationship to others" which "reaches out to the outcast and the dispossessed."[6]

The church's witness to the world is best understood as "pouring out its life to satisfy human need whenever and in whatever form it finds it."[7] This involves both social ministries to the individual and social action ministries to the society as a whole. Bennett states, "The faithful church will cry out for social justice and will attempt to become an instrument of social change that will help to redeem the structures of society and join Christ ministry within the world."[8] He identifies the functions of worship, evangelism, education, fellowship, missions, Christian social ministries, and social action as the minimal requirements for the church "which wants to be found faithful." Miles, however, reminds us that there are some churches that "talk about the full gospel but only offer the priestly half while neglecting the prophetic half of the good news."⁹

The ministry imperatives outlined in Acts demonstrate the nature and mission of the church and serve as a call to be involved in Christian social ministries. See Acts 2:4; 10:28; 10:34–35; 9:36–42, and 11:17. Havlik said it best: "God is always trying to get the church to see where He is at work in the world so that church can join him there."¹⁰

The words of Maimonides, a theological philosopher and physician who lived from 1135–1204 A.D. illustrates historically how God's people were involved in helping the poor. One of his writings was entitled, "The Eight Degrees of Charity." It reads as follows:

1. The first and lowest degree is to give, but with reluctance or regret. This is the gift of the hand, not of the heart.

'2. The second is to give cheerfully, but not proportionately to the degree of the sufferer.

3. The third is to give cheerfully and proportionately, but not until solicited.

4. The fourth is to give cheerfully, proportionately, and even unsolicited, but to put it in the poor man's hand, thereby exciting in him the painful emotion of shame.

5. The fifth is to give to charity in such a way that the distressed may receive the bounty, and know their benefactor, without being known to him. Such was the conduct of some of our ancestors, who used to tie up money in the corners of their cloaks, so that the poor might take it unperceived.

6. The sixth, which rises still higher, is to know the objects of our bounty, but remain unknown to them. Such was the conduct of those of our ancestors who used to convey their charitable gifts into poor people's dwelling, taking care that their own persons and names remain unknown.

7. The seventh is still more meritorious; namely, to bestow charity in such a way that the benefactor may not know the relieved persons, nor the names of their benefactors, as was done by our charitable forefathers during the existence of the Temple. For there was in that holy building a place called the Chamber of the Silent, where

in the good deposited secretly whatever their generous hearts suggested, and from which the poor were maintained with equal secrecy.

8. Lastly, the eighth, and the most meritorious of all, is to anticipate charity by preventing poverty; namely, to assist the reduced fellowman, either by a considerable gift, or a sum of money, or by teaching him a trade, or by putting him in the way of business, so that he may earn an honest livelihood, and not be forced to the dreadful alternative of holding out his hand for charity. This is the highest step and the summit of charity's golden ladder.

THE BAPTIST FAITH AND MESSAGE

A PART OF the biblical and theological grounding for ministry through Christian Women's Job Corps of Woman's Missionary Union, SBC, can be found in Article XV of *The Baptist Faith and Message* adopted by the Southern Baptist Convention on May 9, 1963. While this article is seldom given much public attention, it is nonetheless extremely important to ministry and missions. It is entitled "The Christian and the Social Order." It reads: *Every Christian is under obligation to seek to make the will of Christ supreme in his (her) life and in human society. Means and methods used for the improvement of society and the establishment of righteousness among men (people) can be truly and permanently helpful only when they are rooted in the regeneration of the individual by the saving grace of God in Christ Jesus. The Christian should be opposed in the spirit of Christ to every form of greed, selfishness, and vice. He (she) should work to provide for the orphaned, the needs, the aged, the helpless, and the sick. Every Christian should seek to bring industry, government and society as a whole under the sway of the principles of righteousness, truth, and brotherly (sisterly) love. In order to promote these ends Christians should be ready to work with all men (people) of good will in any cause, always being careful to act in the spirit of love without compromising their loyalty to Christ and His truth.*

(Ex. 20:3–17; Lev. 6:2–5; Deut. 10:12, 27:17; Psalm 101:5; Mic. 6:8; Zech. 8:16; Matt. 5:13–16,43-48, 22:36-40, 25:35; Mark 1: 29–34, 2:3 ff, 10:21; Luke 4:18–21;

10:27–37, 20:25; John 15:12, 17:15; Rom. 12–14; 1 Cor. 5:9–10, 6:1–7, 7:20–24, 10:23–11:1; Gal. 3:26–28; Eph. 6:5–9; Col. 3:12–17; 1 Thess. 3:12; Philemon; James 1:27; 2:8.

The overall purposes and underlying principles of all Christian Women's Job Corps sites are the same. Certainly God is at work through those who have responded to God's Word through their involvement in CWJC, and God continues to bless those who are striving to provide both priestly and prophetic help to women in need.

[1]John F. Havlik, *Where in the World is Jesus Christ?* (Nashville: Broadman Press, 1980), 21.

[2]Robert Morris, *Rethinking Social Welfare: Why Care for the Stranger* (NY: Longman, 1986), 70.

[3]Donald B. Kraybill, *The Upside-Down Kingdom* (Pa.: Herald Press, 1978), 25.

[4]T. B. Maston, *Why Live the Christian Life?* (Nashville: Thomas Nelson, 1974), 120.

[5]Shirley C. Guthrie Jr., *Diversity in Faith: Unity in Christ* (Philadelphia: The Westminster Press, 1986), 63.

[6]Bill J. Leonard, *The Nature of the Church*, vol. 12 of *Layman's Library of Christian Doctrine* (Nashville: Broadman Press, 1986), 27.

[7]Glenn Hinson, *The Integrity of the Church* (Nashville: Broadman Press, 1978), 53.

[8]G. Willis Bennett, *Guidelines for Effective Urban Church Ministry* (Nashville: Broadman Press, 1983), 33.

[9]Delos Miles, *Evangelism and Social Involvement* (Nashville: Broadman Press, 1986), 31.

[10]Havlik, 21.

8
....

The

Rationale

for

Christian Women's Job Corps

The Rationale for Christian Women's Job Corps
by Evelyn Blount

GOD'S TIMING IS PERFECT! Certainly this is true for the beginning of the Christian Women's Job Corps℠. Just look at the evidence: welfare reform (the Personal Responsibility and Work Opportunity Reconciliation Act of 1996) and new legislation affecting volunteers (the Volunteer Protection Act of 1997). The fact that CWJC℠ was already in the pilot stage when the Welfare Reform Act was passed further indicates God's perfect timing. The resources God has provided through Woman's Missionary Union ® for helping women in poverty are also clear indications of God's hand at work in CWJC.

THE NEED
MORE THAN HALF of all families in poverty are headed by women. Many of us could be only one step away from sharing their plight. Did you know that in just a 10-year period about one-fourth of all Americans experience poverty as a result of a local or national recession? These are called the "temporarily poor" as opposed to the fewer than 3 percent who are "persistently poor"—those who live in poverty for more than eight years. For other women and children, serious illness, disability or partial disability, divorce, or the death of a husband can plunge them into poverty.

Many of us have misconceptions about the causes of poverty, especially among women. We have become victims of myths of poverty, when we ought to be motivated to aid women by the facts of poverty. Women in poverty need a hand up, not a handout in order to attain a self-sufficient lifestyle. Contrary to popular opinion, most women in poverty want to work.

According to a 1997 "Report from the Urban Institute," more than two-thirds of women on welfare had some recent work experience before applying for public assistance. About 43 percent of women who receive welfare during a two-year period combine work and welfare to support themselves. So, why are women in poverty? Who are they? Statistics from two CWJC job sites will help replace some myths with facts:

San Antonio, Texas site:

Women on welfare more than two years	18%
Women who lost jobs	3%
Women who are recently separated (usually due to abuse)	24%
Women whose spouses recently lost a job	3%
Women whose spouses are in jail or prison	6%
Women who are underemployed	18%
Women who cannot do former jobs because of illness or injury	27%

York Association, South Carolina site:

Women who quit school, made bad choices in relationships, became pregnant	14%
Women who left abusive husbands	5%
Women who are divorced	6%
Women who are widowed	1%
Women who was abused by father, quit school in the sixth grade, never allowed to leave home	1%
Women born into families living in poverty	3%
Women who quit school and married at an early age, have a husband who is totally disabled, and she cannot support family	1%

Through the pages of this book, the faces of poverty become personal. The stories of Brenda, Elaine, Jean, Amber, Jane, Nancy, Beverly, Cindy, Marsha, and Loretta (not their real names) allow us inside the lives of women in poverty. They help us see there are many reasons why women are in poverty. Many of these women want to work, are willing to work, or are working. They simply do not make enough money to get out of poverty.

In *The Poverty of Welfare Reform*, Joel F. Handler writes that "the 'problem' of welfare dependency is not the recipients...[but rather] the job market and the conditions of work." He further shows that the female workforce, characterized by low wages and little employment security, defies the logic of using welfare to put people back to work.[1]

In a speech at the University of South Carolina, Harvard sociologist William Julius Wilson blamed the state of joblessness for the number of people on welfare. Wilson believes that people on welfare want to work and that joblessness, bad schools, lack of health care, neighborhood instability, and the "enduring burdens" of slavery keep millions of people from rising out of poverty. The fact is that two-thirds of America's poor families include someone who is working.

There are other factors that make an impact on the wages women earn and the job market available to them:

1. Women who are in better-paying, management positions find that there is a glass ceiling which keeps them from advancing to higher management positions.

2. Women who leave the job market to have/rear children find their skills have deteriorated and they have not kept up with technology when they need to or are ready to return to the paid workplace.

3. Women earn less than men do because they perform different work in the economy (occupational gender separation).

4. Employers may also invest less in female workers because they often believe females will not stay as long as

males, thus the return on their investment will not be as great.

5. Women hear about jobs from other women. Men hear about jobs from other men. They use different job networks. Knowledge of available jobs determines who gets them.

6. Women are more likely to work in small firms with relatively low levels of unionization and profit.

7. The entry of women into some formerly male-dominated fields may have devalued work in those fields, and wages have stagnated or fallen.

8. There is a gap in the educational accomplishments attained by women versus men, even though this gap is changing.

Another factor in the number of women in poverty is single parenthood. Single mothers are divorced, widowed, or never married. For those women, getting a job that pays enough to move her family out of poverty is only one concern. Each mother must also deal with the critical role of child-care costs, lack of access to health care, and concern for the emotional needs and supervision of her children.

Adding to the financial stress of single mothers is the lack of or the small amount of child support provided by fathers. According to the findings of the Personal Responsibility and Work Opportunity Reconciliation Act of 1996, 46 percent of female-headed households with children under 18 years of age are below the national poverty level.

At one time, poverty was seen as an urban problem. Today, the rural poverty rate is rising faster than others are. This includes the inner city where there are fewer jobs, lower pay, and transportation costs to the job are higher.

When the Christian Women's Job Corps was being developed and piloted, the figure used most often for the amount of pay per hour needed for a woman to move from poverty to self-sufficiency was a minimum of $7.50 per hour. Early in the pilot stage, that minimum amount proved to be insufficient. Women in poverty are not starting from a debt-free situation; most have debts for life's necessities that can be staggering. According to *Work, Welfare, And Single Mothers' Economic Survival Strategies* by Kathryn Edin and Laura Lein, most single mothers will need $9.00 per hour to pay their bills. In 1997, the federal government's poverty guidelines were as follows (indicated as annual income):

Size of Family Unit	48 Contiguous States and D.C.	Alaska	Hawaii
1	$ 7,890	$ 9,870	$ 9,070
2	10,610	13,270	12,200
3	13,330	16,670	15,330
For each additional person, add	2,720	3,400	3,130

For a family of three in the contiguous states and D.C., income must be $1,111 a month. Maximum welfare assistance for a family of three is $280 a month. In 1997, minimum wage was $5.15 per hour. A total $13,330 a year requires an income of approximately $6.41 an hour. In the United States, about 12.3 million workers earn minimum wage. Of these, 57.9 percent are women. The fastest growing group in poverty is elderly women, and 30 million Americans are without health coverage.

THE LAW AND CHRISTIAN WOMEN'S JOB CORPS

ON AUGUST 22, 1996, President Bill Clinton signed the Personal Responsibility and Work Opportunity Reconciliation Act of 1996 (the Welfare Reform Act). At the signing he said that the Welfare Reform Act should "be remembered not for what it ended, but for what it began: a new day that offers hope, honors responsibility, rewards work, and changes the terms of the debate."

Some critics see the Welfare Reform Act as a cruel, heartless act that will send people who can't help themselves deeper into despair and poverty. For example, Bread for the World (BFW) opposed this legislation. The explanation given by

BFW for their opposition was that the legislation was not real welfare reform.

To support their position, in The 1996 Welfare Law, Lynette Englehardt, BFW policy analyst, said, "It does not provide sufficient funds to help low-income people find good jobs with decent pay and benefits so that they can escape poverty. According to the Congressional Budget Office (CBO), the law falls $13 billion short in funding to put welfare families to work and is $1.4 billion short of having sufficient funding for the child care needed by welfare families alone." This is one main reason why ministries such as Christian Women's Job Corps are needed to help women in need.

The Welfare Reform Act limits the time for receiving assistance to 24 months (2 years) out of each 10 years with a maximum of 60 months (5 years) over a lifetime. There are exceptions, such as for a parent with a child under six. Individual states may lower the time that a person may receive assistance. Each state is given flexibility in implementing this law, which may lead to innovative programs to assist needy people.

Plans adopted by each state decided had to be in place by July 1997. Even though that deadline has passed, people can still be advocates for individuals in poverty by expressing their concerns to their representatives and influencing future welfare plans. All states are required to make their plans available and it is important that each interested person get a copy of their state plan.

Time limits on welfare make CWJC more crucial since its goal to help women find jobs with sufficient salaries to stop welfare assistance. Because CWJC is holistic—spiritual, mental, emotional, educational, and social—it offers women in need support in areas that often keep them from maintaining employment once they have it.

THE WELFARE REFORM ACT

JUST WHAT IS the Welfare Reform Act? What has it done? How does it enable a person to move off welfare assistance? The Welfare Reform Act consists of nine Titles:

Title I	Block Grants for Temporary Assistance for Needy Families (TANF)
Title II	Supplemental Security Income (SSI)
Title III	Child Support
Title VI	Restricting Welfare and Public Benefits for Aliens
Title V	Child Protection
Title VI	Child Care
Title VII	Child Nutrition Programs
Title VIII	Food Stamps and Commodity Distribution
Title IX	Miscellaneous

While each title has an impact on poverty, Title I–Block Grants deals with those issues that make the biggest impact on CWJC. This is seen in the four purposes that are spelled out in Section 401 of Title I–Block Grants. They are:

1. Provide assistance to needy families so children may be cared for in their own homes or in the homes of relatives;

2. End the dependence of needy parents on government benefits by promoting job preparation, work, and marriage;

3. Prevent and reduce the incidence of out-of-wedlock pregnancies and establish annual numerical goals for preventing and reducing the incidence of these pregnancies;

4. Encourage the formation and maintenance of two-parent families.

Family assistance, bonuses to reward decreases in illegitimacy, supplements for population increases, and bonuses to reward high performance states are examples of grants available through this title. Of primary interest is how the grants are to be used. Each state determines part of the use. Any state may use the grant to make payments (or provide job placement vouchers) to state-approved public and private agencies that provide employment placement services to individuals who receive assistance under the state program funded by this part. Vouchers may be certificates, electronic transfers, or other appropriate forms.

Any state may also use the grant to conduct a program to fund individual development accounts established by individuals eligible for the program. To do this, a person must plan to use the account for postsecondary educational expense, a first home purchase, and/or to start a business.

Postsecondary expense may be used for tuition and fees required for enrollment and books, supplies, and equipment required for course work. A qualified educational institution may be a vocational/technical school, college, or university.

Start-up funds are for new, legal businesses. Applicants must have a business plan that includes such things as qualified financing (money from an established financial institution or a nonprofit loan fund having demonstrated fiduciary responsibility), thorough description of the business, and a marketing plan.

A key element of the Block Grant is the Mandatory Work Requirement as defined in Section 407. The federal government has established participation work requirements with which state governments must comply. The participation rate for families receiving assistance is set on a graduating scale beginning with 25 percent in 1997, ending with 50 percent by the year 2002. This figure changes for two-parent families and is 75 percent in 1997 to 90 percent in 1999 or after. The number of hours worked per week in the month varies based, among other things, on the number of parents in the family, health conditions, and the number and ages of the children. A state may exempt a single parent with a child under the age of one from working.

What constitutes work? Section 407 includes 12 activities that are defined as work:

1. Unsubsidized employment.

2. Subsidized private sector employment.

3. Subsidized public sector employment.

4. On-the-job training.

5. Work experience (including work associated with the refurbishing of publicly assisted housing) if sufficient private sector employment is not available.

6. Job search and job readiness assistance.

7. Community service programs.

8. Vocational educational training, not to exceed 12 months for any one person.

9. Job skill training directly related to employment if the recipient has not received a high school diploma or a certificate of high school equivalence.

10. Education directly related to employment.

11. Satisfactory attendance at secondary school or in a course of study that will lead to a certificate of general equivalence.

12. The provision of child-care services to an individual who is participating in a community service program.

Work is such an important part of the Welfare Reform Act of 1996 that on March 8, 1997, President Clinton issued a memorandum to all heads of executive departments and agencies requiring federal agency and department heads to use all available authorities to hire people off welfare rolls. The President had previously called for every church to hire one person off welfare.

Section 104, Title I, is Services Provided by Charitable, Religious, or Private Organizations. This section provides a safeguard that the government cannot dictate to a religious organization if they choose to use funds granted through Title I. The purpose of this section is to allow states to contract with religious organizations without diminishing the religious freedom of the religious institutions. It also says that a religious organization, including a church, "shall retain its independence from Federal, State, and local governments, including such organizations' control over the definition, development, practice, and expression of its religious character."

The law specifies that government shall not require a religious organization to alter its internal governance or remove icons, Scripture, or other symbols. There are the requirements for religious organizations using these funds. No church may discriminate against an individual in providing assistance based on the basis of religion, religious beliefs, or refusal to participate in religious practices. A religious organization must also submit to the same fiscal accountability as other contractors.

This means the organization must account, in accord with generally accepted accounting principles, for the funds provided to the program. However, no other funds, if federal funds are kept in a separate account, will be subject to audit. The religious organization may not use government funds for sectarian worship, instruction, or proselytizing. Simply put, the law sets parameters for the church and government to work together.

Important components of the Welfare Reform Act are related to child care: responsibilities of parents, including requiring fathers to support the children that they helped to bring into the world and for fathers to be educated to the need for providing child support; child protection and child nutrition programs. There is a definite shift in this new law from elderly to children. This will especially benefit single mothers.

THE VOLUNTEER PROTECTION ACT
ON JUNE 19, 1997, President Clinton signed into law H.R. 911, The Volunteer Protection Act of 1997. According to Representative Bob Inglis, Congress of the United States, who worked with John Porter (R–IL) to get the bill passed, "The bill contains three important provisions designed to clarify the liability of volunteers of nonprofit organizations:

1. Volunteers won't be liable for actions they take in good faith. To get this protection, volunteers must have acted with good intention within the scope of their responsibilities as a volunteer. However, if volunteers cause harm by willful or criminal misconduct, gross negligence, or reckless misconduct, they don't receive any protection.

2. Individuals who commit hate crimes, violent crimes, sex crimes, or who violate the civil rights of others, don't receive protection. Volunteers who cause harm while under the influence of alcohol also don't get protection.

3. Since tort law has traditionally been a state responsibility, the bill allows states to opt out if they choose not to adhere to these standards.

What does the bill do? It encourages "the State to enact legislation to grant immunity from personal civil liability, under certain circumstances to volunteers working on behalf of nonprofit organizations and government entities." Many states have already enacted laws granting protection to volunteers. It is important to know what these laws are.

The door has been opened for Christians and their churches. The time is right to become advocates for and participants in aiding women in poverty. Christian Women's Job Corps has come into existence for such a time as this. Fellow Christians, we must walk through the door.

WOMAN'S MISSIONARY UNION

WOMAN'S MISSIONARY UNION has many resources and attributes that uniquely qualify the organization to help women in poverty. As the name implies, WMU is predominantly an organization of women. Women identify with women. Even when there are vast differences between them, there is a bond that calls women to come to the aid of other women.

One of the greatest resources of WMU is the network that is already established. Through local church, association (county), and state WMU leadership, women across America are known by name; their gifts, talents, and skills are identified; and their addresses and phone numbers are available. Because of the network that is already established, in a short time, WMU can organize and motivate the volunteers to provide the needed services to help women in poverty or at risk of poverty. In rural and urban settings and from Baptist churches with fewer than 50 members to churches with thousands of members, the WMU organization is already established, leading WMU members and the church to be involved in and to support missions. (Missions is what the church does to fulfill the Great Commission—it is taking the love of Jesus Christ to persons not related to the church or its programs through ministry and witness.)

From the beginning of its existence, WMU has raised money for missions. Whether local, associational, state, North American, or international missions is involved, WMU has been at the forefront raising the funds needed for the Southern Baptist missions enterprise. The organization is applying these same principles and channels for fund-raising to CWJC.

Training women is important to the ministry of WMU. Even before WMU had a national organization, women at the local church, association, and state levels were training women to be leaders and to participate in missions. Specific training events and resources are provided to develop leadership skills. Training exists in areas as varied as working cross-culturally, planning for budget development and accountability, teaching reading and writing or English as a second language, understanding stress and ministering to people in stress, or developing ministry skills required by the specific area of need.

In addition, as age-level organizations were added, leadership development was built into the structure. According to age-level characteristics, members are given leadership roles—from choosing individual and group activities as preschoolers and children to having responsibility for planning studies, activities, and ministries as teens and adults. Leaders and members identify the potential in women and are willing to do what is necessary to develop that potential.

Finally, WMU has a history of being involved in combating social and moral problems. Even the forerunners of WMU—Female Missionary Societies, Female Mite Societies, Dorcas Societies—were involved in ministry in their local communities. Whatever the missions issue of the day, WMU was involved. From teaching slave children to read and write, to ministering to people with AIDS and their families; from working to change child labor laws to working with economically disadvantaged; from assisting immigrants to leading the denomination in addressing race relations, WMU members have been making a difference in the lives of people.

As early as 1909, Personal Service became a department in the national WMU organization. The official WMU Plan of Work from 1914 to 1960 included the following statement: "We declare ourselves in sympathy with all the forces of righteousness: international and interracial justice; world peace; patriotism; national prohibition; Christian Americanization; universal education; Sabbath observance; sacredness of the home; the family altar; high standards for womanly speech, dress, and conduct; improved industrial conditions; child welfare; public health." From early beginnings until now, WMU has added missions-related social and moral issues as they have emerged. Built on a solid foundation through WMU, CWJC is proving to be a well-organized, holistic, effective ministry effort that is making a world of difference—one woman at a time.

¹Handler, Joel F., *The Poverty of Welfare Reform* (New Haven: Yale University Press, 1995), 177.

Epilogue

EPILOGUE

HAPPY BIRTHDAY CHRISTIAN WOMEN'S JOB CORPS

ON MARCH 1, 1998, CWJC was officially one year old. Like any newborn, the first year of life was highlighted with firsts!

• The first client graduated from a technical school on the dean's list.

• The first graduate returned to CWJC to be trained as a mentor.

• The first CWJC participant became self-sufficient.

• The 175 men and women successfully completed the first National Certification Training.

• The first CWJC video, *Christian Women's Job Corps: From Dependency to Self-Sufficiency*, produced by Stan Hill, was honored with a Silver Angel in the 21st Annual International Angel Awards sponsored by Excellence in Media, an entertainment industry foundation based in Hollywood that was established to recognize those productions with a moral or social impact.

• The Literacy Council of San Antonio honored CWJC with a Life Long Learning Award.

• The South Carolina CWJC program received public endorsement from that state's governor.

• The York County CWJC site was approved as a field placement site for social work students from the University of South Carolina as well as Winthrop University.

• In March the Alabama Restaurant Association assisted in training Birmingham's Southside CWJC participants and placed 11 graduates in jobs within the food service industry.

• CWJC's nomination for the Action Institute for the Study of Religion and Liberty's Samaritan Awards won the runner-up distinction for Woman's Missionary Union.

A CHALLENGE TO REMEMBER

YOU THE READER have already met Evelyn Blount in the pages of this book. You have read that she was present at the meeting in Dallas, Texas, where the Christian Women's Job Corps concept was born and that she serves on the national task force. You have learned from her as you read her rationale for this ministry of WMU. And now you know of her involvement in the development of CWJC in South Carolina. Evelyn is undeniably a credible spokeswoman for CWJC! When interviewed for the award winning video *Christian Women's Job Corps: From Dependency to Self-Sufficiency*, she was asked what about the idea of CWJC particularly appealed to her. Evelyn's response speaks eloquently to the remarkable story of CWJC: "To me it is the single most comprehensive approach that Southern Baptists have ever had to meeting the needs of people."

In his 1998 best-seller, *The Street Lawyer*, author John Grisham allows his reader access to the emotional roller coaster and life changing experiences of Michael, a successful Washington, D.C. lawyer, whose life is impacted by his relationships with homeless individuals and families—people in need. In one chapter, the reader joins Michael at the morgue as he identifies the bodies of Lontae Burton and her children. "I closed my eyes and said a short prayer, one of mercy and forgiveness. Don't let it happen again, the Lord said to me."[1]

Lontae would have been a candidate for Christian Women's Job Corps. And while Grisham's homeless mother is fictional, our cities and counties are populated with homeless women, women in poverty, and women in need. Indeed, we must not let these women be forgotten ever again. Together we must continue to multiply CWJC sites and thus increase the remarkable story of God at work in this life-changing ministry.

---

[1]Grisham, John, *The Street Lawyer* (New York: Doubleday, 1998), 94.

HOPE FOR THE FUTURE

IT WAS OUT OF her love for the Lord, her obedience to Him, and her desire to ensure the future development of CWJC that Edythe Oulliber, in September of 1997, joyfully wrote the first check to the WMU Foundation to begin a Christian Women's Job Corps Endowment Fund. Edythe vows her support of CWJC is not linked to her daughter, Trudy Johnson, CWJC national director. Instead her belief in this biblically based, holistic ministry inspired her giving so that generations to come will be no longer forgotten—CWJC will be there to minister to their needs.

Tax-deductible donations may be made to the Christian Women's Job Corps Endowment Fund through the WMU Foundation, P. O. Box 11346, Birmingham, AL 35202-1346.

A PLACE FOR YOU

THERE IS SOMETHING that everyone can do to be involved in Christian Women's Job Corps!

Christian Women's Job Corps
A Ministry of Woman's Missionary Union

I think it's the most exciting thing that's happened in my lifetime. As far as the church, as far as Woman's Missionary Union, and as an opportunity to really be the church of Jesus Christ in the world. —Evelyn Blount